BILL MASON

WILDERNESS ARTIST

from heart to hand

Rocky Mountain Books
#108—17665 66A Avenue
Surrey, BC V3S 2A7
www.rmbooks.com

Edited by Alister Thomas
Book design by Janine Vangool
Front cover: Bill Mason at Denison Falls on Ontario's Dog River, circa 1980. Photo by Becky Mason.

Printed and bound in Hong Kong by Book Art Inc., Toronto

Rocky Mountain Books acknowledges the financial support for its publishing program from the Government of Canada through the Book Publishing Industry Development Program (BPIDP).

Library and Archives Canada Cataloguing in Publication

Buck, Ken, 1944-
Bill Mason, wilderness artist : from heart to hand / Ken Buck.

Includes bibliographical references and index.
ISBN 1-894765-60-5

1. Mason, Bill, 1929-1988. 2. Influence (Literary, artistic, etc.)
3. Wilderness areas in art. 4. Artists--Canada--Biography. 5.
Motion picture producers and directors--Canada--Biography.
6. Canoeists--Canada--Biography. I. Title.

ND249.M373B82 2005   709'.2   C2005-903912-4

To family and friends

But ask the animals, and they will teach you,
or the birds of the air, and they will tell you;
or speak to the earth, and it will teach you,
or let the fish of the sea inform you.
Which of all these does not know
that the hand of the Lord has done this?
In his hand is the life of every creature
and the breath of all mankind.

The book of Job 12: 7-10
Quoted by Bill Mason in *Waterwalker*

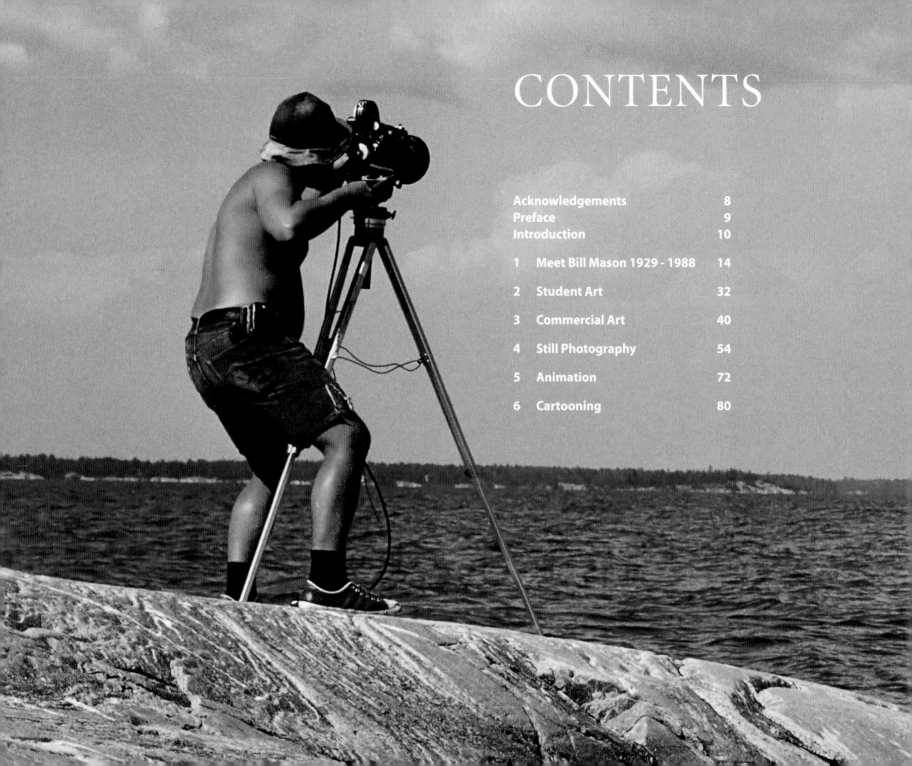

CONTENTS

Acknowledgements   8
Preface   9
Introduction   10

1   Meet Bill Mason 1929 - 1988   14

2   Student Art   32

3   Commercial Art   40

4   Still Photography   54

5   Animation   72

6   Cartooning   80

7   **Sketches and Paintings**   **92**

8   **The Storyboards**   **122**

9   **Films**   **138**

10 **Behind the Scenes**   **194**

11 **Cameras and the art of seeing**   **206**

12 **The Final Films**   **210**

13 **The Studio: A Cabin in the Woods** **214**

Bibliography and Filmography   **216**
Relevant Readings   **219**
Index   **220**

*Ken Buck filming
the Mason family
on Georgian Bay in
1974, Photo by
Susan Buck.*

Acknowledgments

Preparing this book was a life-altering experience. Rarely do you have the need, or the opportunity, to revisit your past in such detail. I was frequently overcome by waves of comprehension about important events in my life. Sometimes strong emotions were rekindled . . . as if thirty years had not passed. Some conversations replayed in my mind . . . as if they had been recorded on tape. Sometimes I could feel the camera in my hands and the spray from Lake Superior on my face . . . but always I was reminded of my tremendous good luck to have been a part of Bill Mason's career and to have such close bonds with his family.

Our first shooting trip (from left): Bill Mason, Joyce Mason, Becky Mason, Paul Mason, Ken Buck and Susan Buck. Georgian Bay, 1970.

Joyce Mason, together with Paul and Becky, gave me unstinting support and encouragement in completing this book. They opened Bill's studio and all his artwork without questions or limitations. My wife Susan showed infinite patience and support, not to mention a razor-sharp editor's eye.

Many friends were recruited to proofread all or part of the book. I valued all opinions and recommendations. Some suggestions altered tone and nuance; others grew into entirely new topics that I had somehow overlooked. As a retired English teacher, it was a humbling experience to have my grammar and spelling under such close scrutiny—all for the better. Lloyd Seaman, a true stickler for spelling, punctuation, grammar and syntax, rescued me from my own prose. Wally Schaber found major omissions and had countless details to fill out the story. Wally also encouraged me to introduce this project to the public at his annual Trailhead Outdoors Show in 2004, with the positive response encouraging me to complete the book.

James Raffan gave generously of his time and encouragement to this project and also contributed valuable research and insightful perspective. Bill Burr was one of my earliest readers and consequently had an even more daunting task than the others, and I thank him for persevering. Joyce, Paul and Becky reminded me of many details of our experiences. Don and Willy Campbell welcomed me into their home and filled in many details about Bill's early years as a commercial artist. Bill's

sister and her husband, Elizabeth and Dave McKenzie, provided some of Bill's early art and many good stories. And finally, thanks to the Bone Marrow Transplant team and the staff in the Medical Day Care Centre at the Ottawa General Hospital without whom there would not have been enough time. To all these generous people, and to all the other contributors, thanks from this searching biographer.

Preface

Even before Bill was finished making his series of wolf films in the late 1960s, he was lobbying the National Film Board of Canada to give him a new project. He wanted to make an instructional film on canoeing. He decided to film the annual Mason family canoe trip in 1970, down the French River from Lake Nipissing to Georgian Bay, as a pilot to help sell the idea. At the time, Becky was six years old and Paul was eight. Bill invited Susan and me to be a volunteer crew, and we leapt at the chance.

Susan and I had moved to Meech Lake two years earlier and we got to know the Masons quite well. I had helped Bill with the endless chores that came with having a pack of wolves in his backyard. Sometimes I actually had time to do some filming in the wolf enclosures. Susan and I were both teachers and free for the summer, and we loved the adventure of filming a wilderness canoe trip. So the four adults and two kids set off in two canoes. The trip was memorable for many reasons. Susan and I had just invested in a new 16-foot Chestnut Pal canoe and a new Baker tent. We were anxious to try them out on their first real trip. And best of all, we were going to do some shots for Bill.

The footage we got that summer was a great success. The pilot was convincingly beautiful and entertaining, and Bill was awarded a contract to make the *Path of the Paddle* series.

For my part, I fell in love with filmmaking. It was the perfect job and so exciting to see the rushes two or three weeks after we got back home. From the start, I felt that the camera was a natural extension of my own interests. It seemed like I had finally arrived at my destination even though I had not specifically set out to get there. Watching a story unfold at the movies had always fascinated me. In high-school art classes I learned about perspective and composition, and I had explored photography with the only camera I could afford—a little Kodak Instamatic. I was a camper and canoeist. I had no idea that these skills and interests would converge, with opportunity thrown in for good measure, but they did.

On location for Waterwalker *at Lake Superior Provincial Park in 1971. Bill's canoeing season ended only when the lakes froze over.*

I was woefully uneducated in any formal way to take on the job of professional cinematographer. But I was keen and Bill taught me so much. After that first summer of shooting, I went back to teaching high school full-time. However, my appetite for filmmaking had been whetted. I had a new ambition.

During the next couple of years I worked for Bill as a second cameraman and a general gofer on weekends and holidays. It was a good arrangement, but it was also frustrating for Bill as the canoe project was fast becoming much bigger than he had anticipated. He needed more help. Bill convinced the National Film Board to hire me on contract. They were reluctant to do so, though by then, with two Oscar nominations in his portfolio, Bill had enough clout to get what he wanted.

So, in the spring of 1974, I resigned from the Ottawa Board of Education and began working for the National Film Board, a cultural institution admired around the world. I knew that this was a great new beginning; I was sure that I would never step back into the classroom again.

One successful canoe film led to another. It took 10 years to make all six canoe films. I worked full-time with Bill for two-

and-a-half of those years, 1974 to 1977. I also worked part-time for the next six years for Bill and as a freelancer on other projects. Between contracts in 1977, I went back to teaching high school just "for a few months" . . . and stayed for 21 years.

I spent hundreds of hours with Bill driving to locations, canoeing through wilderness and working in the studio. We filled the hours with conversation about everything: our childhoods, our families, our values, our work, our concerns for the future. As good friends do, we tested our perceptions of the world on each other. Sometimes we just travelled in comfortable, happy silence. This book is really just an extension of those conversations, illustrated by Bill's art and photographs.

Ken Buck

Bill Mason slipped his canoe into the early calm; the canoe cut silently through the water and was swallowed up by the mist. The sun was just breaking over the forest walls, creating a diffused light illuminating emerging details along the shoreline. Soft silhouettes of trees took shape overhead. This was not a shot in one of his famous canoe films. For Bill it was just another day at the office, or to be more precise, another day of commuting to the office.

It was 1958 and Bill had just moved to Ottawa to work as an animator for Budge Crawley. It was Bill's plan to rent a cottage at Meech Lake, but nothing was available, so he set up camp on the north side of the lake and commuted by canoe and car to Crawley Film Studios in Ottawa every day for about six months. This was Bill's idea of heaven—to be able to commute to work by canoe. Fortunately one of Mel Alexander's log cabins came up for rent, allowing Bill to move under a roof for the winter. Actually, he would have been glad to stay in the tent, but he also got engaged to Joyce Ferguson that year, and he needed a home for his bride. They lived at Meech Lake from 1959 until he died in 1988. He was just 59.

Bill went on from Crawley Film Studios to become one of Canada's most prominent documentary filmmakers. Through his films he became a powerful champion for environmental activism in Canada, and indeed the world. He was driven by a sense of duty to rescue the environment in general, and the wilderness in particular, from predatory and unsustainable misuse. All his films, but especially his two documentary feature films, *Cry of the Wild* and *Waterwalker*, were enchanting and entertaining, yet they carried a weighty subtext about environmental responsibility. It was through his stories that he put Canadians in touch with the Canadian wilderness and showed them why they should care about it.

At this writing it's been 16 years since Bill Mason died of cancer. The fact that his name, his films, his books and his influence have endured is a testament to his creative genius in combining storytelling, art, entertainment and ethics. His ideas, provocative and progressive at the time, have proven to be wise and insightful, underpinning our current collective sense of environmental ethics.

Few people have had the influence that Bill Mason had in shaping the Canadian identity. His films, produced at the National Film Board of Canada, have been mainstays in Canada's schools for the last 40 years. Educators have used *Paddle to the Sea, Rise and Fall of the Great Lakes, Wolf Pack, Death of a Legend, Path of the Paddle, Face of the Earth* and many others to introduce generations of students to Canada's wilderness and the concept of environmental stewardship. Bill's vision of the wilderness as benign, beautiful and precious effectively offered a meaningful alternative to the accepted cultural perception of wilderness as something to be feared, conquered or exploited.

Since some of Bill's films were autobiographical, he became a familiar face to many Canadians. Bill rose in prominence, perhaps even to celebrity status, just before the great boom in high-tech camping equipment and canoes. His was a Romantic persona, a woodsman from an earlier era—complete with Woods #1 canvas canoe packs, green corduroy pants and woolen plaid shirt, moccasins and black toe rubbers, a cotton Baker tent and wooden canoes. As one admirer said, "He was the kind of canoeist every Canadian would like to be for at least one canoe trip in his life."

In his youth, as Bill became more and more attuned to and committed to environmental responsibility, he used his art to pass on that message, taking every opportunity in his commercial art and photography to introduce Canadians to their own wilderness.

The single most compelling force behind Bill Mason's passion for keeping the wild in wilderness was his deep unwavering Christian faith. He believed that man did not have "dominion over," but "responsibility for" the world. God did not create the world for man to abuse it, to exploit it, to destroy it. Man must nurture it. Bill's art was a fusion of faith, art, action, honesty, pragmatism and fine craftsmanship.

His commercial art, created in the 1950s and '60s, sold product and taught lessons in Canadian history and environmental ethics at the same time. His clients provided Bill with a platform from which he could advocate his vision. Like the best teachers, the main point of Bill's lesson was represented in unspoken analysis and reflection. In all his films he used this multi-layered agenda of entertaining and teaching. And often the most important part of the lesson remained unexpressed but perfectly clear.

After graduating from the University of Manitoba and starting his commercial art career, Bill was able to go on extended canoe trips, sometimes for months at a time, ending only because of freezeup. He often canoed solo despite the well-intentioned objections of just about everybody. It was during these extended one-person trips that Bill had plenty of time to contemplate our place in nature. He could not look at untouched wilderness without the sure knowledge that it would inevitably be sacrificed to progress. The more he fell in love with the wilderness, the more determined he became to protect it.

During these trips Bill shot still photographs, using a medium-format Rolleiflex camera. He edited and assembled his slides into presentations for friends, colleagues, church

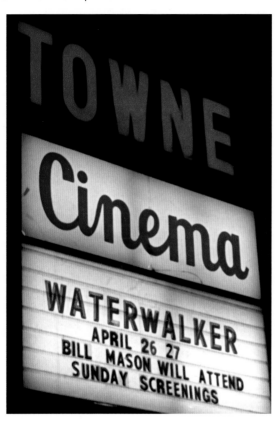

A Bytowne theatre marquee in Ottawa, 1986.

Bill Mason at his Meech Lake studio easel, 1980.

groups and students. He felt that if he showed people the beauty of the wilderness, they would inevitably become responsible environmentalists.

His slide show, *The Timeless Wilderness*, connected Bill to his first film job. In 1956 a young Toronto-based filmmaker, Chris Chapman, had a contract to make a film about Quetico Provincial Park. He needed an assistant who knew how to live in the wilderness and play the part of the canoeist. He heard about Bill from someone who had seen *The Timeless Wilderness*. Chris hired Bill, allowing one great Canadian documentary filmmaker to launch the career of another.

Bill's rise to success as a filmmaker was meteoric. The first film he made for the National Film Board of Canada, *Paddle to the Sea*, won 11 awards and was nominated for an Academy Award (Best Short Film) in 1968. One of life's little ironies: he lost to his mentor, Chris Chapman's *A Place to Stand*. In 1970 Bill was nominated for a second Academy Award (Best Short Film) for his documentary, *Blake*. By the mid-seventies Bill had become one of Canada's most successful documentary filmmakers.

Bill's influence was not confined to Canada, with most of his films translated into several languages. Queen Elizabeth showed *Paddle to the Sea* at one of Princess Anne's birthday parties and then wrote Bill to express her pleasure at how well the film was received by the children.

Every Canadian who is a canoeist or an environmentalist will be familiar with Bill Mason's name. His favourite Prospector canoe shares a display area with former Prime Minister Pierre Elliott Trudeau's birchbark canoe in the Canadian Canoe Museum in Peterborough, Ontario. His films were consistently among the 10 most frequently rented films from the NFB. For several years he had four films in the top 10—an amazing feat. He acquired 28 international film awards, and in 1974, was accepted into the Royal Academy of Arts for his artistic mastery of the film medium.

In 1983 Bill retired from filmmaking to pursue his first love: painting. He had been experimenting with a technique for several years, applying oil paints to paper with a palette knife. Bill's exploration of this technique played a major part in his feature documentary film, *Waterwalker*. When it was completed, Bill was ready to strike out in a new career as a professional painter. For a few short years after he retired from the NFB, he divided his time between writing three books and painting. But in 1988 Bill's career as a painter was cut short by his untimely death.

Many words have been published about Bill's life and works, however, an artist's story is not complete until it is told through his art. The legend of Bill Mason is best illustrated and understood by seeing examples of all of his work. His commercial art, still photography, films, books, cartoons and paintings collectively tell the story of the artist. His art inspired many Canadians to become environmentalists. His canoe films invited a whole generation to get in touch with their cultural roots by travelling and living in the wilderness. Seldom has a Canadian artist held the hearts and minds of so many admirers, shaping and defining what it means to be Canadian. And few people of any nation have been so influential in creating a sense of responsibility for the environment.

Bill Mason, Cape Gargantua, Lake Superior, 1980.

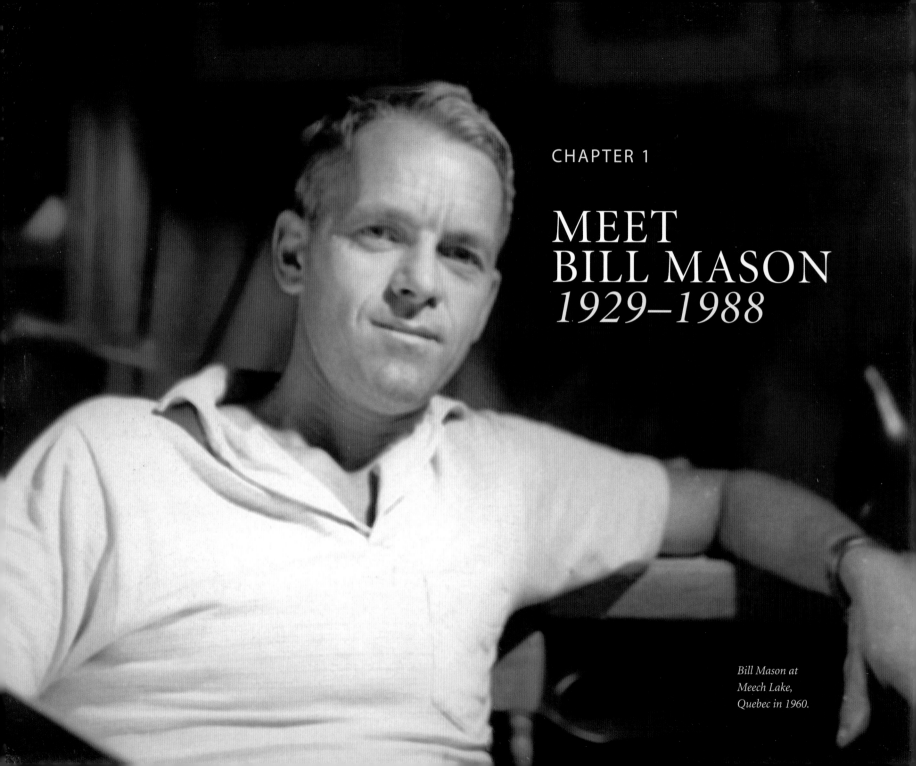

CHAPTER 1

MEET
BILL MASON
1929–1988

*Bill Mason at
Meech Lake,
Quebec in 1960.*

Beginnings

William Clifford Mason was born into a modest Winnipeg household on April 21, 1929. His father, William Sr., a clerk for the Great West Life Assurance Company, married Sadie Fair in 1928. Bill was the eldest of two children; his sister Elizabeth was seven years younger.

While Bill became one of Canada's most influential advocates for environmental issues and one of this country's most successful documentary filmmakers, he was, above all, an artist. As a child he had art projects on the go all the time, such as drawing and making model villages, complete with people and things sculpted of Plasticine.

Although his parents, friends and teachers recognized Bill's remarkable artistic talents, he struggled with schoolwork, partly due to his many absences. He was frequently ill with allergies. As he explained in his film, *Waterwalker,* "… they flunked me in grade 1 because all I would do was draw canoes. But I knew that I didn't need all that school stuff because I already knew what I was going to be — a canoeist and an artist. Look who's laughing now. Now I make my living being a canoeist and an artist."

He thrived when school projects

Bill, at about 18 months, in Winnipeg.

involved artistic talent since no matter what the assignment was he turned it into a beautiful work of art or a carefully crafted design. He spent the last year of high school in a personalized program supervised by the art teacher, Miss Carey, and graduated in 1950 from the University of Manitoba School of Art with a diploma in Commercial Art.

Bill, 10, and his sister, Elizabeth, 3, in Winnipeg.

Grand Beach, Lake Winnipeg

ABOVE
Handwritten on the back of this picture: "Already we couldn't get him out of the water." So began a life's work centred on water.

ABOVE RIGHT
The Coney Island atmosphere of Grand Beach was an odd place to begin a lifelong love affair with wilderness and solitude.

The most formative and important experiences in Bill's childhood were the annual summer holidays at Grand Beach on Lake Winnipeg. Bill's Grampa Fair rented a cottage every summer, eventually buying his own. Every summer the Masons and Fairs joined the exodus north from Winnipeg by train to Grand Beach. It was in the carnival atmosphere of this small-town resort and holiday retreat that Bill learned to love water, nature and canoes.

Those summer days, especially with his Grampa Fair, formed some of Bill's happiest childhood memories. It was at Grand Beach where Bill saw his first canoes—the rentals tied up at the dock at Nelson Boat Livery. He was fascinated with the canoes, sitting in them for hours, dreaming about glorious wilderness adventures and freedom. William Sr. rented a canoe several times a summer for one hour at a time. These moments only increased Bill's appetite for more.

One summer the family could actually afford to rent a canoe for a week, so Bill felt like he actually owned it. William Sr. and Bill paddled up and down the shores of Lake Winnipeg, never leaving sight of town. These simple excursions provided Bill with some of his fondest recollections of time spent with his father.

If you want a boat, build one

Bill continually had some project on the go. One of his most ambitious, as a 12-year-old, was constructing a kayak out of plywood. Anyone who has tried to build a boat of any kind knows full well the difficulties, but Bill succeeded . . . and it floated.

This resourcefulness, craftsmanship and determination prevailed in all of Bill's later endeavours—if he needed something he would make it. But what was the point of having a kayak if you couldn't use it? Incredibly, Bill received permission from his parents to paddle the homemade kayak on the Red River, which was just around the corner from their home, and

FAR LEFT
Bill built this plywood kayak in the backyard at 209 Oakwood Avenue when he was just 12. His parents allowed him to camp overnight on the banks of the Red River with this boat. He returned the next morning elated by the experience.

LEFT
Bill found good use for his homemade kayak during the Winnipeg flood of 1950. Unfortunately his family lost many of their treasures, including almost every piece of art that Bill created as a child and young man.

even more astonishingly, to camp out overnight. These were major concessions from his parents who were protective of their son, especially as a result of all his health problems. Bill could never explain why they allowed him to do such a "weird" thing. But they did.

It was one of the great turning points in his life. His mother, recollecting years later, said Bill was on cloud nine talking about the river, the camping, the birds and the animals. Bill remembered an overriding sense of freedom.

Decades later, after he retired, Bill made a dock chair which still sits on his dock at Meech Lake. Designed with a solid high back to protect the sitter from a wind blowing down the lake, Bill cobbled it together from found materials left over from building his house. Big enough for two and with broad arm rests wide enough to hold tea, cookies, books, pencils and paper, the remarkable quality of this backyard marvel was how comfortable it was to sit in. Its clever design actually extended the dock-sitting season by many days as the sun warmed you on one side and the wind couldn't get at you from the other. Bill spent hours in this chair writing his books, and just escaping.

Growing up small

Bill was beset with health problems most of his life, which was quite surprising to anyone who knew him — he appeared to be tireless and robust in everything he attempted. Physically, he was strong, skiing all day then playing hockey for two hours that night. Professionally, he juggled several projects at one time with apparent aplomb. But behind the tough, wiry little man lay the constant battle with childhood allergies, a life-threatening heart attack at 36, and a nagging, debilitating digestive problem his whole life. Eventually duodenal cancer killed him.

Bill was always small in stature — at 17 he looked like he was 12. While his classmates towered over him, it must have been a psychological burden, the ever-dynamic Bill was popular, often the organizer of neighbourhood games.

Bill and his buddy Blake Herman at Grand Beach, Manitoba. Bill's classmates and friends often soared over him, but Bill made up for his small stature by being enthusiastic. Being different from everyone else was actually one of Bill's valuable characteristics in later life.

Bill, as a university student, at his drawing board.

Even when Bill started at the University of Manitoba, he was short and slight. As a last resort, his parents took him to the Mayo Clinic in Rochester, Minnesota, where he was diagnosed as a slow starter but normal. In spite of this, the doctors gave Bill growth hormone drugs, and by the end of his three years at university, he filled out to a whopping 135 pounds on a 5-foot-5 frame.

There is some speculation that Bill paid a high price for this growth spurt. The drugs may have exacerbated his allergies, and perhaps, even compromised his health, leading to his otherwise inexplicable heart attack.

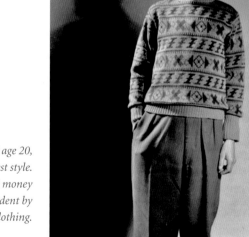

Bill, about age 20, in the latest style. He earned money as a student by modelling clothing.

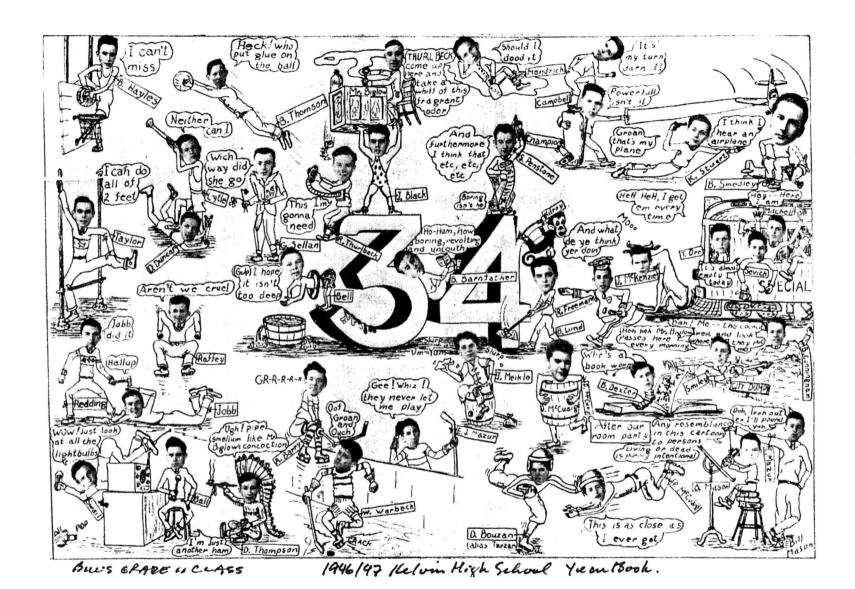

Kelvin High School Year-book, 1946-47

Every year Bill drew caricatures of his classmates, much to their delight and dismay.
Bill included himself, in the lower right-hand corner sitting on a stack of books, in this Grade 11
class collage. His sense of humour was already apparent in this collage, but his cartooning style
evolved in later years.

A lifelong hockey career

Bill's passion for hockey was evident throughout his childhood, lasting his entire life. He spent many hours playing pick-up games at the Riverview Community Centre rink, where he organized the kids to shovel the rink and then play for hours at a time. Some of Bill's better childhood memories of his father were from the hockey games they played together in Winnipeg.

Forty years later, Bill was still the mastermind behind pick-up games on Meech Lake, on his own backyard rink or in Ottawa arenas. When Meech Lake froze over early in the winter, Bill called everybody he knew to play shinny. Sometimes there were 30 players on a rink the size of three football fields. When the inevitable snow fell, the games shifted from the lake to Bill's backyard rink, which was about one-quarter the size of a National Hockey League ice surface. Games went on for hours, punctuated by tea breaks.

Like the boy in his painting, *After the Game* (now displayed in the trophy cabinet at the Riverview Community Centre), he was forever counting his goals and kibitzing with the other players. When his son Paul began to play with him they had heated season-long scoring races, keeping accurate count on their kitchen calendars. Bill was so proud of Paul when he and his buddies could finally take Bill into the boards and really push him around on the ice.

CLOCKWISE FROM TOP LEFT: Bill lacing up for Crawley's hockey team in Ottawa, circa 1960. Bill playing pick-up hockey as a kid in Winnipeg at the Riverview Community Centre rink, circa 1940. Bill and Paul in their backyard rink, with one of the few goalies who made their team. Members of the Trail Head Blades, Ottawa. Bill Mason and Wally Schaber modelling the latest in hockey uniforms and stick/paddles at Meech Lake.

Christianity, religion and life at home

William Mason, Sr. was volatile. He clung to his job at the Great West Life Assurance Company, desperately glad to have work during the Great Depression when so many around him were unemployed. His dogged determination to provide for his family in the face of dire times reflected a determined Presbyterian stoicism.

But after the Depression and World War II, William Sr. grew bitter and obsessive about being trapped in a job that he hated. His disappointment with his own life did not make for a happy home. He was often angry and sometimes went on drinking binges, something that Bill never forgot nor forgave.

As Bill became successful, William Sr. became jealous, resentful and bitter. Even after Bill had been twice nominated for an Oscar at the Academy Awards, William Sr. could not find any joy in his son's success.

However, it was William Sr.'s mother, the Bible-quoting tyrannical matriarch, Granny Mason, who was the major influence in Bill's life. She controlled everything in her household and in William Sr.'s life.

Granny Mason had an inexplicable control over her daughter-in-law, Sadie (Fair) Mason. Every day Sadie walked several blocks to Granny Mason's house to clean, cook, iron, preserve and obey any whim that came into Granny's mind. Granny, who confined herself to her chair when it was convenient, nurtured an imaginary illness, using it as an excuse to make Sadie take care of her.

Granny Mason was an adamantly outspoken enemy of alcohol and its consumption. Yet, she convinced herself that the only medicine that could save her was . . . brandy. And only the best brandy: Courvoisier. She sent William Sr. to buy it, something he could ill afford. When he tried to pass off cheap brandy by putting it into an empty Courvoisier bottle, which she had just finished, she went into a rage. She heaped guilt on him for not loving her, risking her health and not doing his Christian duty. Then she sent him back to the liquor store for the expensive stuff.

Her hypocrisy was an example, in Bill's mind, of inexcusable manipulation and exploitation. It served Bill well. He learned how hypocrisy can poison and destroy people, both the perpetrators and the victims.

Bill's life was a conscious and deliberate rebellion against the religious excess and hypocrisy he saw around him. This intense and determined rebel abhorred self-deceit and selfishness, resisting being held a slave to the opinions of neighbours as well as self-serving interpretations of the Bible.

In spite of all these constraints and negative influences, Bill did not turn his back on religion, Christianity or the church. He was committed to Christianity, remaining so his entire life. In fact, he was determined that his faith would liberate him, not confine him.

Out of this decay of the human spirit grew these great constants in Bill's life: his Christian faith, his determination to be an artist, his love of wilderness and canoeing, and his determination to never allow the same negative influences to affect his own family. All of Bill's life's work was grounded in his faith.

He found a mentor in Dr. Fred Mitchell, pastor of Elim Chapel in Winnipeg, where Bill went to church. It was Dr. Mitchell who introduced Bill to the idea that the King James Bible interpretation of "dominion" in the book of Genesis was misleading. It should be read as "responsibility." This became a cornerstone of Bill's philosophy on environmental issues.

Bill was active in the Elim Chapel's Young Peoples' Club. For years he attended and led Bible study classes. And at Kelvin High School, he was involved with the Inter-School Christian Fellowship and later the Inter-Varsity Christian Fellowship. In later years Bill invited the local chapters of IVCF to his house at Meech Lake to play hockey, watch films, and almost as an afterthought, to discuss the Bible.

It took some time, and hard lessons, for Bill to drop the evangelical enthusiasm with which he approached his art. It quickly turned people off. His best work occurred when he buried the evangelism into subtext, presenting an overtly secular message.

Manitoba Pioneer Camp and teaching

Manitoba Pioneer Camp, located just east of Winnipeg on Shoal Lake, was established by the Inter-Varsity Christian Fellowship to provide a summer camp for youth in a Christian environment. Bill heard about it when Wilber Sutherland, an IVCF director, came to speak to the Young People's Club at Elim Chapel. The same year, 1944, Bill's Grampa Fair reluctantly sold the cottage at Grand Beach, so Bill, then 15, persuaded his parents to let him go to camp. It was his first experience away from home and his first formal instruction in canoeing skills. It was a perfect match for Bill.

Manitoba Pioneer Camp became the centre of his life as he returned the next year as a counsellor-in-training and every year after that as an instructor and guide until he moved to Ottawa in 1958. Over the years, Bill, affectionately known as "Paddles" Mason, was instrumental in changing its focus from a waterfront camp to a wilderness tripping camp.

The first film that Bill made, *Wilderness Treasure,* was sponsored by Inter-Varsity Pioneer camps. The co-producer was Wilber Sutherland, who became one of Bill's closest friends and was instrumental in making Bill's *Waterwalker* some 25 years later.

It was at Manitoba Pioneer Camp where Bill matured as an instructor and teacher. He learned from Fred Mitchell that good teaching is organized and enthusiastic sharing of interests and knowledge with others. This is how Bill, who was always disarming and engaging, with a folksy and unpretentious public speaking style, relayed his messages at camp and in all his films, lectures, books and paintings.

TOP *One of Bill's fun things was to teach campers how to sail a canoe. He remained an avid canoe-sailor all his life. Indeed, a most memorable scene is the sailing sequence in* Song of the Paddle.

ABOVE *Bill (in the hat) led canoe trips all summer at Manitoba Pioneer Camp.*

ABOVE *Bill, canoe guide and camp counsellor at Manitoba Pioneer Camp on Shoal Lake, circa 1956.*

The artist as a young man

Bill enhanced his reputation as an outdoorsman and a wilderness artist when his story appeared in the Star Weekly magazine in 1958. The similarities between the article and the Waterwalker film, 25 years later, are remarkable.

To no one's surprise, Bill became a talented commercial artist, and after graduating from art school, he was hired by the Winnipeg art house, Phillips, Gutkin and Associates. Bill thrived there, making lifelong friends with Don Campbell, Blake James and Barrie Nelson. Reluctant to commit himself to a full-time, nine-to-five job, Bill invariably asked for the summers off to go canoeing. PGA always said "no," so Bill quit amid howls of protest from his more sensible employers and family. He went canoeing for weeks, sometimes months, and when he returned PGA hired him again. Bill was too good a talent to lose, even though he had the disquieting habit of quitting for half-a-year at a time.

Bill's parents were never supportive of his aspirations to become an artist. While they respected his artistic abilities, they did not approve of his career choice. Bill's mother Sadie was especially distressed by his "irresponsibility," finding his behaviour incomprehensible and dissolute. Later, when Bill suffered a heart attack, she blamed the event on his "sinful" lifestyle.

Ironically, Bill's mother was a capable landscape painter in her own right. Nonetheless, she couldn't comprehend how anyone could make a living at art. She asked Bill: "It's nice that you got a job at the art house, but when are you really going to start working?" As Bill met with one success after another, it didn't seem to make any difference to his parents. They never saw filmmaking as a real job that a responsible adult with a wife and two children would do, especially when it involved working with wolves in the backyard. Sadie, in her later years, eventually conceded that "Billy" had done well.

Bill's extended canoe trips quickly evolved into painting and photography expeditions. Don Campbell, a professional photographer at PGA, convinced Bill to buy a Rolleiflex camera, known for its reliability and sturdiness. He taught Bill how to use it and they went on many wilderness trips together, spending hours, sometimes days, setting up shots. When Bill travelled alone, he rigged up ingenious remote controls so he could be photographer and subject at the same time. Early on, he constructed a slide show, *God's Grandeur*, which he showed to service and church groups all over Winnipeg.

A special role model for Bill was Tom Thomson, the highly acclaimed Canadian landscape painter and mentor to many of the Group of Seven, who died under mysterious circumstances in 1917. In addition to admiring his work, Bill felt his life had strong parallels to Thomson's: both were commercial artists who kept their dreams of painting alive while doing work-a-day commercial contracts; both left sensible jobs to canoe alone in the wilderness; both felt compelled to celebrate the beauty of the natural world in their art.

A book that caught Bill's eye was Sigurd Olsen's *The Singing Wilderness*, published in 1956 and which resonated with Bill's intuitive love of the land. Of particular inspiration were the book's pen-and-ink illustrations by Francis Lee Jacques. Taken together, they encouraged Bill to record his own wilderness experiences in drawings.

Bill learned most of his practical wilderness skills from Calvin Rutstrum's books, *The Way of Wilderness* and *Paradise Below Zero*. Rutstrum was a great champion of the campfire or Baker tent which became Bill's trademark tent.

Star Weekly special

The *Star Weekly* magazine, based in Toronto, published an account in 1958 of Bill's solo trip on the north shore of Lake Superior. Rutstrum's Baker tent, which captured heat from a campfire burning in front of it, was featured prominently in the article. Even today a Baker tent, made of waterproof Egyptian cotton, will turn heads; it is remarkable how many people identify it as a Bill Mason tent, and will start up a conversation asking if the owners knew Bill. Unfortunately it is almost impossible now to buy a Baker tent. Even Bill had to get his custom-made by Black's Camping Stores in Ottawa.

CLOCKWISE FROM TOP LEFT Fishing just above Cascade Falls at the mouth of the Cascade River. Reading maps for the next day's journey by candle light. Wild columbine. Bill Mason, young artist and outdoorsman. Bill pitched his Baker tent out on a point for the view and the wind on the north shore of Lake Superior.

It was a very good year:
Joyce Ferguson, Crawley Film Studios
and Meech Lake

Bill was offered a job in Ottawa as an animator at Crawley Film Studios, one of the most successful film houses of the day. The year was 1958, and even though he moved to the nation's capital, Bill's employer in Winnipeg, the advertising agency Paul, Phelan and Perry, kept him on as art director.

In keeping with his "outrageous" lifestyle, Bill camped on the north side of Meech Lake in Quebec's Gatineau Hills. This necessitated canoeing to the road to reach his car, and so began the commute to Crawley's, a daily trip that Bill loved. Later that year he rented a log cabin at the lake. He had found his home; he would live there for the rest of his life. And his steady income at Crawley's made another life change possible.

A year later, in 1959, Bill married Joyce Ferguson, a student nurse he met through Elim Young Peoples'. For their honeymoon they took a cross-Canada working holiday filming *Wilderness Treasure*, living out of their car and sleeping in a tent.

Both sets of parents were not amused by this bohemian, unanchored way of life. Finally Bill and Joyce made it back home to Meech Lake. Once again their parents considered this an uncivilized situation — living in a "shack." It didn't help matters that Bill's livelihood was drawing animated cartoons. It was beyond the imagination of family and friends back in Winnipeg and, truth be told, that was exactly how Bill and Joyce liked it.

Joyce oversaw Bill's life. She was his bodyguard, setting up a friendly but impenetrable barrier around Bill when he was working. Because he worked from home, many people didn't grasp the fact that he could not be interrupted when he had deadlines. Joyce was the final critic on every film he made and book he wrote. She was his touchstone with reality, tempering his manic work ethic. During breaks in the morning and afternoon, Bill could escape the editing table and wind down for fifteen minutes with tea and cookies at the kitchen table. Joyce reported on his many phone calls and Bill chose the one that he *had* to answer. Then he would make that small journey back to the studio, which was a million miles away from the comfort of Joyce's kitchen.

ABOVE LEFT Bill and Joyce sailing on Meech Lake in one of his 23 canoes. One way of escaping the demands of their exhausting work loads, and the incessant phone calls, was to get out in the middle of the lake.

ABOVE Bill and Joyce making maple syrup, the quintessential Canadian spring ritual. For years the neighbours on Meech Lake, led by the tireless Grant Crabtree, collected sap and boiled it to make maple syrup. This annual ritual was a great social event for marking the end of winter. However, the syrup making was often interrupted by the spring's first descent of a local river or creek by canoe.

LEFT Bill, Joyce, Paul and Becky on Meech Lake, about 1965.

FAR LEFT Bill and Joyce at their first home at Meech Lake, a log cabin they rented from Mel Alexander, a descendent of the family who owned the original Alexander Ski Lodge at Meech Lake.

LEFT Bill's trademark "hockey paddle" marked the entrance to his driveway at Meech Lake for years.

Home: Meech Lake, Quebec

Bill and Joyce lived at Meech Lake for three decades, from 1958 to 1988. During that time he helped shaped Canadians' understanding of their own land, challenging them to love it as much as he did. His life as an artist celebrated the timeless wilderness and the wilderness treasure.

LEFT Bill and Joyce built their first home, a log house, in 1984 at Meech Lake. Bill hung a birchbark canoe over the door, and in the backyard, built a canoe shed for about 25 boats, depending on how carefully he arranged them.

A lifetime of sharing and teaching

Bill's instinct for teaching was pure and uncluttered by other agendas. Still, he had one underpinning topic: responsibility for the environment. Like most excellent teachers, he was a natural storyteller and raconteur, loving to teach because he loved to share.

Bill shared all his skills—from starting a campfire and building an igloo to making a film and writing a book. These skills enabled students to live fuller and better lives, to be creative, and maybe, to be an artist. Bill also shared the intangibles: the glory of a misty-morning dawn on a wild river, the awesome power of moving water, the fragility of a river, the inexplicable beauty of a canoe slipping through the water.

Bill admired the work of William Blake (1757—1827), the English poet, painter and prophet. In his poem *Auguries of Innocence*, Blake expressed the same wonder that Bill had about seeing God in nature:

> *To see a world in a grain of sand*
> *And a heaven in a wild flower,*
> *Hold infinity in the palm of your hand*
> *And eternity in an hour.*
> (Lines 1—4)

Bill understood perfectly the Romantic definition of a transcendent experience: The knowing of God's power and love is made possible by understanding that His genius, the glory and the love can be seen in a dragonfly's wing.

Bill never heard the last of this one! He met the Bucks and Meldrums by chance at Warp Bay on Cape Gargantua, Lake Superior. He had dashed out on short notice to record some sound and, to save time, had thrown all his gear into cardboard boxes. He forgot his pots and pans, so he had to borrow from us. We made him pose with our kids demonstrating how to camp out of cardboard boxes. From left: Ian Buck, Peter Meldrum, Bill, Joey Meldrum and Jenny Buck.

From the family album

LEFT *Paul takes a nap on a nice soft thwart.*

BELOW *Joyce and newborn Paul.*

NEXT PAGE, CLOCKWISE *Becky fetching water, Georgian Bay, 1970. Happiness is a frog in a bucket. Becky and Paul in the waves at Georgian Bay, 1971.*

ABOVE *The liftover, paddling with one-year-old Paul.*

RIGHT *Becky in a multiple exposure taken at night by Bill, circa 1985.*

CHAPTER 2

STUDENT ART

The artist as a student: the early years

The Masons abandoned their home in 1950 when the rampaging Red and Assiniboine Rivers overflowed. Never before had the spring flood waters done serious damage to the Mason house (just a few inches in their basement), but this time the water rose to the first floor. The Masons left Bill's artwork on a table in the basement assuming that the water would never get that high. Unfortunately it did, and this time most of his art was reduced to sodden ruins. On the bright side, Joyce and Bill's sister, Elizabeth, still have a few pieces that somehow escaped the water.

Bill was an art student from the day he started kindergarten. In fact, there was never a time when he didn't know that he would be an artist. His ability to draw bailed him out of many problems in his academic courses, often submitting beautifully rendered projects instead.

Bill excelled in art class and throughout his school years he lived for the art room. In his last year at Kelvin High School, Bill was given a special timetable where his home room was the art room, meaning he spent most of his time there. Miss Carey, the art teacher, made invaluable contributions to Bill's art skills and his education. At home he always immersed himself in an art project. Only hockey in the winter and trips to Grand Beach in the summer could interfere with his art.

Before Bill graduated from art school he committed himself to fine art lessons, forever whetting his appetite to be a painter. Bill seemed quite willing to accept the role of art student in the classic sense—the best way to become an artist is to study the masters who went before you.

In his younger years, Bill had romantic notions about the wilderness, frontier days, voyageurs, and cowboys and Indians of the pioneer days. William Sr. encouraged Bill to do paintings of the Wild West. Since praise was rare in the Mason household, Bill, imitating the style of Frederic Remington, the American painter and sculptor (1861 - 1909), accommodated his father by drawing stereotypical Hollywood Indians.

Yellow Cottage, circa 1950. Oil on canvas (10" x 8"). Private collection.

Head of Man

Celebration of the natural world and an obsession to protect it did not become the great driving force in Bill's art until he had more experience in the wilderness. His days at Manitoba Pioneer Camp and his ever-more adventurous canoe trips awoke in him a deeper understanding of what wilderness really was, and what it meant to him.

Finding his artist's voice

As a student Bill divided his attention between two artistic disciplines: fine art and commercial art. Ultimately he knew that commercial art would be his life.

Bill's early work as a student showed a good grasp of perspective, texture, anatomy, drama and colour. He was capable of producing technically accomplished work in all his art-school assignments, thriving on exploring many styles. But he was always in search of his own signature style, one that would set him apart.

As much as he admired Thomson and the Group of Seven, he certainly didn't want to copy them. For Bill, art was a constantly evolving form, infinite in its variety but borne out of the past, so he looked to the masters for inspiration on his own artistic journey.

Bill took photographs to prepare for his studies of mass and power. His fascination with perspective is obvious in both the photography and artwork.

He thought that Walt Disney's use of perspective in animated films was brilliant. Every time Disney Studios released a new animated film, or re-released one of the great animated classics—*Pinocchio, Snow White, Fantasia, Cinderella*—Bill went to see it, preferably with some kids.

PREVIOUS PAGE
Lombard Street
Flood, *Winnipeg,
1950.*

*Repairs after the
flood, circa 1950.*

CLOCKWISE
The Yards, *circa
1954. Oil on board
(12" x 16"). Private
collection.*

The Counterweight
and Train, *circa
1954. Oil on board
(12" x 16"). Private
collection.*

*Bill used a photo
study of a train and
bridge counterweight
(above) as a reference
to produce the
painting at left. This
was the massive
counterweight on
the bridge over the
confluence of the
Red River and the
Assiniboine Rivers in
Winnipeg, Manitoba.*

Bill had never been to Arizona, but he had seen many Westerns that were filmed there. Some of his early influences are evident in these early works, such as Hollywood Westerns, Frederic Remington and the Group of Seven. Bill's eclectic early art suggests that there was a mighty search—for a style, a subject, a raison d'être—going on within him. He was entranced by heroic figures and deeds. Hollywood movies filled him with romantic, but needless to say, totally skewed visions of the wilderness, the frontier and Indians. Textbooks fed his imagination about the fur trade, the voyageurs and the *coureurs de bois*. The Hudson's Bay Company, after all, had its headquarters in his hometown. However, it took a long time to sort out reality from boyish adulation.

By the early '60s Bill knew that the style he was developing was not what he wanted. He found his early work embarrassing in its naïveté, describing it as lifeless. He also discovered the reality of how the fur trade had disastrously exploited the native people, his idealistic notions of the frontier replaced by a more realistic understanding of history. He began to travel in the wilderness, discovering still photography under the guidance of Don Campbell.

RIGHT Rooftops in Winnipeg, *circa 1950. Oil on board (12" x 14"). Private collection.*

BELOW Fishing boats at Grand Beach, *circa 1950. Oil on board (12" x 14"). Private collection.*

And he discovered J.M.W. (William) Turner, a great 19th century British painter. It was a combination of Turner's fascination with light and water and use of palette knives and glazes that inspired Bill. After he and Joyce saw Turner originals at the Tate Gallery in London, England in 1970, Bill felt that Turner had shown him a path to follow. Yet, it still took about 20 years for Bill to feel that he had actually even come close to understanding Turner's technique, let alone develop it into his own style.

Assignments from art classes

RIGHT
Trompe d'oeil, *circa 1950. Watercolour on paper (10" x 14"). Private collection.*

BELOW RIGHT
Study in Red, *Black and White, circa 1950. Watercolour on paper (10" x 14"). Private collection.*

Art class exercises were far removed from Bill's interests in the wilderness, frontiers and heroic figures, but they offered opportunities to explore alternative styles and topics. Bill actually used all of these techniques in his commercial art.

Bill felt that an artist had to earn the right to be iconoclastic, irreverent, outrageous or avant-garde. He had no aspirations to be iconoclastic, but he did aspire to be a catalyst for understanding who and what we really are. He frequently cited the fact that Picasso could render perfectly conventional and realistic images, and consequently, his abstract art was a legitimate exploration of shape, form and colour. Bill had little patience with pretense, presumption and posers.

"Drawing constitutes the source and substance of painting, of sculpture, of architecture and all other kinds of art."

– Michelangelo

CLOCKWISE

Trompe d'oeil, *circa 1950. Watercolour on paper (10" x 12"). Private collection.*

Bookcase, Manitoba Legislature, *circa 1950. Pen on paper (8" x 12").*

Column segment, *circa 1950. Pen on paper (11" x 14").*

Banister and staircase, Manitoba Legislature, *circa 1950. Pen on paper (14" x 11").*

These studies in pen and ink are part of a series that Bill drew in art school assignments. In his mind all art was grounded in the ability to draw, a full understanding of anatomy and mastery of perspective.

CHAPTER 3

COMMERCIAL
ART

Working for industry

Bill loved commercial art as a business and a way to make a living, but he never gave up on the idea that he would someday be a successful painter. After all, his hero, Tom Thomson, had succeeded in both.

As Bill became more concerned about environmental issues, he recognized that some of his clients did not share his concerns. Many of his employer's clients were involved in enterprises that were detrimental to a healthy environment—the pulp and paper industry, automobile companies and tire manufacturers. But he recognized the reality that he could not turn down customers just because he didn't like what they were selling.

Bill felt like an undercover agent for the burgeoning environmental movement. He developed a voice in his advertisements, usually from one of his passions—wilderness, camping, hockey, Canadian history, the art world—to deliver a message to buy bread, tires or a car.

Whenever possible, Bill tried to work into his ads a "subversive" message about the environment or Canadian history. As he became more successful and influential in the advertising world, he was given more and more freedom to follow his interests and instincts. Clients, like Reimer Express Lines, loved this approach. So, even when Bill was developing advertising for trucking firms or tire manufacturers, he contextualized the client's message into a larger understanding of the natural world.

When he moved to Meech Lake, Bill was far removed from the advertising offices in Winnipeg. James Raffan, author of the Bill Mason biography, *Fire in the Bones*, said this distance from day-to-day scrutiny freed Bill to be even more inventive in his commercial art.

Courtesy of Cooper Tires Ltd.

In this print ad for Cooper Tires, Bill used an animation technique for painting the clouds and stars on glass. The blue-black background was on a second plate of glass, with the trucks on a third. The three plates were then sandwiched together. Many years later he used the same technique in his canoe films to illustrate water flowing in rapids.

Working for the logging industry

Bill also designed ads for the pulp and paper industry. On one hand, he saw this industry as an enemy to the environment. On the other hand, he understood the need for such businesses, and that the people who worked in them were good, hard-working citizens doing the best they could for their families and communities. Bill didn't feel this industry was bad, wood and paper are everyday necessities, after all; it was the unbridled pursuit of company profits at the expense of the environment that was the problem, aggravated by the failure of government to manage natural resources and to regulate industries.

Bill, always professional in his work, was a valued employee at Phillips, Gutkin and Associates and later at Paul, Phelan and Perry. It was not until he finally established himself as one of Canada's premier filmmakers with the National Film Board that he could afford to retire from commercial art. Nonetheless, he always thought of his career as a commercial artist as a valuable, and necessary, stage in his professional development.

Bill was torn about accepting the commission to design a Christmas card for E.B. Eddy, the giant pulp and paper company. He was ready to acknowledge that there was nothing inherently wrong in cutting down trees; the problem arose from corporate and government policies on how the logging was to be done. Long before it was fashionable, Bill supported selective cutting instead of clear cutting by heavy machinery. He also advocated allowing forest fires to run their natural course in the interest of keeping the forests healthy—a radical notion in those days, but prophetic as it turned out.

United Grain Growers: a voice of agriculture
In support of a populist movement

Bill knew how to romanticize nature, farming, the voyageurs and hard labour. Nevertheless his idealizing never became saccharine or maudlin. The drama in this monochromatic rendering of the plowman and his horse celebrates western agriculture, independence and self-reliance. The tiny buildings under the horse's hooves are emblematic of man's relative insignificance in the vast prairies, and yet the lone plowman accepts the daunting task of breaking the soil. The washes and white highlights in this illustration (14" x 20") are stark, stoic and spartan. There is courage and heroism in this depiction of man's struggle to wrest a living from the land.

Bill saw little difference between political, social and environmental responsibilities, as witnessed by this ad campaign for the United Grain Growers. Bill sold the grain growers' message as an important force advocating social justice on the prairies, underscoring that message by celebrating our history and reminding us of those principles that transcend politics and profit.

Whereas Bill was apolitical, not championing any political party, he was a friend of Prime Minister Pierre Elliott Trudeau. They canoed together on several trips, and Trudeau invited Bill and Joyce to formal dinners at 24 Sussex Drive as representatives of Canada's artists. Early in their marriage, Pierre and Margaret Trudeau played broomball at the Mason home on Saturday nights. A few years later they and their young toddlers would drop in on the Masons on their way to and from the prime minister's retreat at Harrington Lake during maple syrup season. Bill and Pierre Trudeau shared a love of

Bill made a series of 10 posters, each with an inspiring quotation, celebrating agriculture and the family farm. The fact that he chose the quotations as significant statements about Canadian culture offers some insight into what he held important.

A VOICE OF AGRICULTURE

"Now, when across the continent we've
seen our task expand,
To our children's children and their
children's children,
We do bequeath this land."

Robert K. Kernighan
'Pioneer's Anthem' 1925

Since 1906, United Grain Growers has
championed the rights of the Canadian
farmer . . . . A Voice of Agriculture.

UNITED GRAIN GROWERS LTD.

CALGARY · REGINA · WINNIPEG · SASKATOON · EDMONTON

Tools were made,
And born were hands
Every farmer understands.
William Blake

Since 1906, United Grain Growers
has championed the rights
of the Canadian farmer

UNITED GRAIN GROWERS LTD.
CALGARY · REGINA · WINNIPEG · SASKATOON · EDMONTON

A VOICE OF AGRICULTURE

Praise be to barns,
Praise to their mighty roofs,
Praise their stout floors
That echo to wide hoofs;
Praise generous doors
Silos like flanking towers
Cart sheds, hen roosts, corn-cribs-
Attendant powers!

Elizabeth Coatsworth

Since 1906, United Grain Growers has
championed the rights of the Canadian
farmer . . . . . A Voice of Agriculture.

UNITED GRAIN 🦅 **GROWERS LTD.**
CALGARY · REGINA · WINNIPEG · SASKATOON · EDMONTON

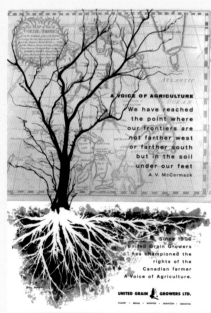

A VOICE OF AGRICULTURE

'To be born on a farm is the greatest
good that can befall a human being'
Peter McArthur
'Around Home'
1925

Since 1906, United Grain Growers has
championed the rights of the Canadian
farmer . . . . . A Voice of Agriculture.

UNITED GRAIN 🦅 **GROWERS LTD.**
CALGARY · REGINA · WINNIPEG · SASKATOON · EDMONTON

A VOICE OF AGRICULTURE

We have reached
the point where
our frontiers are
not farther west
or farther south
but in the soil
under our feet
A. V. McCormack

Since 1906,
United Grain Growers
has championed the
rights of the
Canadian farmer
A Voice of Agriculture.

UNITED GRAIN 🦅 **GROWERS LTD.**
CALGARY · REGINA · WINNIPEG · SASKATOON · EDMONTON

wilderness and canoeing; they also shared a sense of responsibility for the natural world, but they seldom talked politics.

With the exception of a few politicians, Bill felt they were all involved in one way or another in exploiting natural resources. He did not blame them as much as he blamed our culture. Bill's messages in his art encouraged a sense of personal responsibility for the environment, inviting those in power to take actions that transcended mere politics. This campaign for the United Grain Growers was the closest he ever came to publicly endorsing a political philosophy.

History and heritage in advertising

Bill never missed an opportunity to use advertising campaigns to teach Canadians about their history, their ancestors, their place in the environment. Much to Reimer's credit, the company went along with Bill's ideas. In "The Romance of Canadian Transportation," the poster was folded like a road map with only the title panel showing. As you unfolded the poster, each mode of transportation was revealed in chronological order. The struggles of the cartoon figures in their primitive forms of transportation stood in stark contrast to the photograph of the Reimer truck. This visual surprise made the truck and the company name more memorable.

DOG SLED

Some innovations in the transport industry were discovered quite by accident. The first refrigerated transport service was the inevitable result of trying to ship blubber across the frozen Arctic terrain. But dog sleds, and many of the other means of transport then in use, often got lost enroute, so someone thought of trying the . . .

TRAVOIS

Simplicity was the key-word here, just a couple of poles pulled behind a horse with the goods of commerce slung between. Then came the white man who was quick to recognize a functional craft in the form of the . . .

CANOE

For many decades the daring voyageurs paddled their fur laden canoes along the lakes and rivers of Canada's wilderness. Many a canoe and all its crew were lost in rapids or the huge waves of Lake Superior. If the goods did arrive at all, they were often in a pretty soggy and battered condition. Items too large or heavy for canoes to handle were shipped via . . .

COVERED WAGON

In their day, covered wagons, which often travelled at speeds in excess of ten miles per hour, were considered breathtakingly fast. The sight of flying hooves and spinning wooden wheels raising a cloud of dust made everyone watch in awe. For those Western settlers not quite so daring of spirit, there was always the . . .

RED RIVER OX CART

These creaking, groaning vehicles never gained a reputation for speed. In fact, this could be where the saying "as stubborn as an ox" originated. But progress moved on, and soon, the latest word in shipping was the . . .

YORK BOAT

Longer, wider and virtually unsinkable, these craft carried bulky goods of all descriptions up and down Hudson Bay tributaries as far South as the "Red River Settlement". But their size also made it impossible to navigate on smaller rivers and creeks. Meanwhile, shippers who wanted to stay dry used the . . .

TRAIN

Since trains were restricted to following the "ribbon of steel", shippers could be sure that goods wouldn't go miles off their path. These smoke belching "iron horses" played an important role in the development of Canada. When Henry Ford began tinkering around with horseless carriages, a new method of shipping was born . . .

HIGHWAY MOTOR TRANSPORT

It took a while to get the motor transport industry started, but pioneers in the field kept at it. Year after year, improvements were added, until one day there was . . .

REIMER EXPRESS

The unreliable vehicles of earlier days were replaced by powerful new diesels. Driving a transport was no longer an adventure but a "profession" that demanded skilled operators. Now, shippers had greater assurance than ever before that cargos would arrive at their destination safely, on schedule.

Courtesy of Reimer Express Ltd.

IN THE TRADITION OF *Canada's Trail Blazers*

Bill successfully created an image of Reimer Express as a strong, dependable, Canadian company. By including Reimer in Canadian history, the voyageurs in particular, the company was seen as a nation builder. This two-colour brochure had a green-black cover, giving no hint about the client's name. It opened on one fold to reveal the blue-black image that was twice as big as the cover. The only mention of Reimer was an understated sign on the cab's roof. The text made a direct comparison between the heroic efforts of the voyageurs to deliver the goods and Reimer's commitment to get the same job done.

But the age of transporting goods by Canoe has long since gone. Today, one Reimer Express Highway Transport can haul as much in a single trip as 4 to 5 Canots de Maitre handled in a season.

Yet the spirit of Canada's Pioneer Trail Blazers still lingers on. Regardless of conditions or circumstances, it is the special pride of Reimer Express to deliver the goods — as promised. This was the driving force behind those legendary Voyageurs of yesteryear . . . as it is our philosophy today.

When this nation was in its infancy the internal movement of goods was handled by birch bark canoe. Large 35' to 40' "Canots de Maitre", as they were called —regularly operated in the ice-free months between Montreal and the Lakehead. Styled after the Indian War Canoe, these huge Freighter-Canoes would carry from 4 to 5 tons each and boasted a 14 to 16 man crew. In Western Canada, the smaller 25' North Canoe was used, paddled by 6 or 8 men.

Courtesy of Reimer Express Ltd.

In his many ads for trucking firms, automobiles and tires, Bill often used the history of transportation to make a point about his clients' services. But rather than a dry history lesson, Bill used humour to make the connections.

It was Bill's sense of humour that made so much of his work compelling, including his films and books. Bill's ability to draw cartoons and caricatures was the perfect way to get a chuckle out of any audience. Bill captured folly, frenzy and fanaticism in his cartoon characters, making people to laugh at their own silliness or eccentricities. His characters made it obvious that, with a little bit of thinking, people can choose to do things differently—like calling Reimer Express or Allied Van Lines.

Courtesy Allied Van Lines Ltd.

PULLING UP STAKES ?

For early settlers, it was "westward ho" in the rumbling Red River Ox cart!

Take moving today – how easy, safe and smooth it is. With *Allied* service – the dream that became a reality – you spin your telephone dial – your moving worries vanish!

When you move, call your *Allied* agent. There are over 100 agents in Canada with offices linked by teletype and listed in your yellow pages.

The First – the Biggest – the All-Canadian Van Line

ALLIED VAN LINES LTD.

Courtesy Allied Van Lines Ltd.

A love-hate relationship with cars

Bill's friend and mentor Chris Chapman drove a Land Rover, impressing Bill so much that this giant workhorse became his dream car. Bill eventually bought his own Land Rover, the image fitting his lifestyle perfectly: hardy wilderness filmmaker who arrives in places where no one else can go (because they don't drive a Land Rover) to capture the great outdoors on film for his expectant audience. To add to the mystique, Bill had at least one canoe on top of the vehicle . . . just in case. Unfortunately that dream became a nightmare as the Land Rover caused him no end of trouble and expense.

Badly bruised by this dose of reality, Bill thereafter bought the cheapest and oldest cars he could find, ruthlessly, and with great pleasure, driving them into the ground. He screwed hand-crafted canoe carriers right into the roof of the car. And when the car wasn't roadworthy anymore, he rigged up a homemade snowplow to keep his driveway open.

Perhaps the fantasy car on page 51 best exemplifies Bill's attitude towards automobiles and advertising. This model was not a Ford Maverick; it was specially designed by Bill to be a no-name car for use as a prop in his film, *Blake*. The Ford Maverick had yet to be dreamt up by Ford car designers, let alone produced.

Bill had some fun with this little prop. The copy in the ad stated what real car ads only dared to imply in the subtext: car manufacturers sell cars as extensions and enhancements of the macho male ego. Bill realized he had succumbed to the cachet that comes with owning a Land Rover, and was largely laughing at himself in this ad, as well as taking a swipe at the advertising world.

Bill with his latest design in high-tech roof top carrier, probably the Mach VII model. All his inventions were "Mach" something.

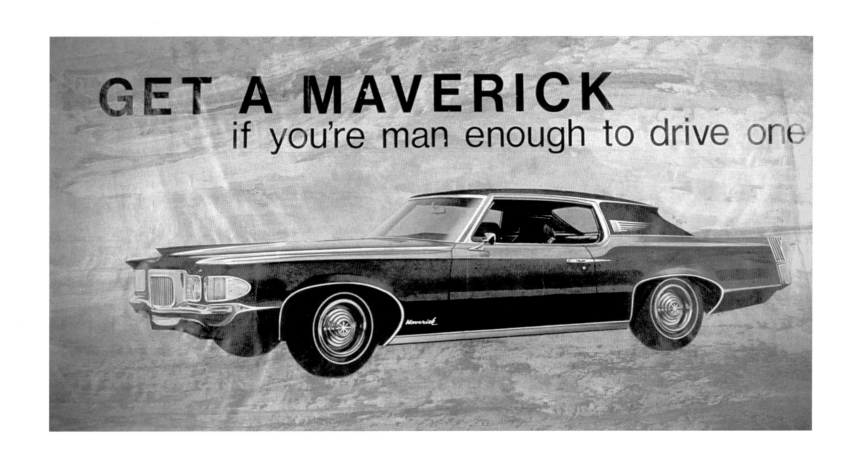

This little dog was one of Bill's favourite stars in his advertising campaigns. Bill had an uncanny ability to embody human folly, suspicion, skepticism and annoyance in the dog's facial expressions, an enviable artistic strength. He was constantly bemused by interactions between pets and their owners, and in his animator's imagination he always saw the owner being controlled by the pet.

Executive position

Bill's job title at Paul, Phelan and Perry Ltd. was art director, so it was necessary to have a formal photograph for the company's annual reports. Fitting the corporate mould, Bill posed as the well-dressed executive. He always got a kick out of the photo, exactly the image his employers, and especially his parents, always wanted him to be.

When James Raffan visited Bill's elderly mother, he noticed a framed picture on her bureau. In spite of all the great dramatic pictures of Bill as an outdoorsman, the only photo she had of her "Billy" was as a suit-and-tie executive. It must have given her great comfort.

When Joyce was making arrangements for Bill's funeral in 1988, she had Bill wearing his flannel plaid shirt and green corduroy pants. He never wore suits, so Joyce found it totally inappropriate to send him off in one. Still, Joyce's mom was shocked and distraught at such a breech of protocol, even though the casket was closed during visitation and the service. Once again, and for the last time, Bill and Joyce broke the rigid conventions of his childhood environment.

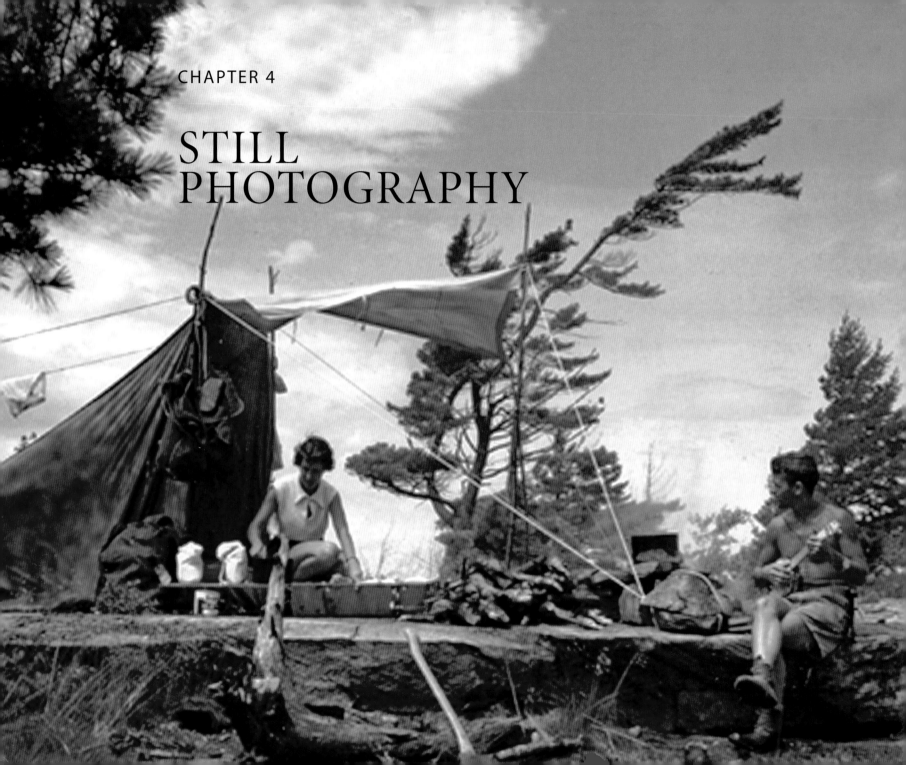

CHAPTER 4

STILL
PHOTOGRAPHY

The Timeless Wilderness

When Bill started to work at Phillips, Gutkin, the ad agency, he was introduced to the art and craft of professional photography. Don Campbell, an accomplished staff photographer, became one of Bill's closest friends, advising him to buy a medium-format Rolleiflex (2.25" x 2.25") as his first camera. It was Don who taught Bill the fundamentals of film as well as the technical side of cameras and lighting.

Bill's training at university and his natural sense of composition and colour made him an apt student. He made photography look easy. You might wonder how he could get it so right every time, but Bill's "out boxes," which are still stored in his studio, tell a different story. For every perfect picture that Bill had in a slide show, there were four or five failures of the same shot. It was only when you saw all the rejected slides that you could get a glimpse into Bill's mind—almost hear him explaining why five versions were unacceptable, yet one was just right.

Bill accumulated an impressive collection of professional quality images, putting them together in a slide show. This was one of Bill's early, and important, learning experiences on his way to becoming one of this country's great documentary filmmakers and storytellers. Sometimes he called the show *God's Grandeur*, other times *God Revealed*. The title accurately reflected Bill's goal. While the topic was the wilderness as God's handiwork, the purpose was to celebrate God's infinite power and generosity in creating such a world.

His presentation worked well provided that he was showing it to a group of Christians who wanted to explore nature as God's handiwork on earth. For any other audience the slide show was overwhelming in its proselytizing and evangelical fervour. Bill was doctrinaire, complete with Biblical references and quotations, chapter and verse. The slide show was a variation and an extension of the Young People's Bible study evenings that Bill led at Elim Chapel.

This was where the learning part started for Bill. Many of his friends, especially the new ones he was making in the business world, came to only one show, never to return. Some, including Don Campbell, told him they loved the images but the religious message was just too overwhelming. Bill was advised to tone it down. He realized that he had to choose between making an overtly Christian message and a secular message based on his Christian principles.

Georgian Bay, 1970.

The title slide for Bill's show was an early example of drawing on glass. Bill, obsessed with maps and aerial shots, included maps with animated overlays in many of his films.

The timeless wilderness

Defining man's relationship with the natural world

Bill's sense of composition and lighting is well illustrated in this shot, with the frame dramatically divided in half: the top half is empty and still, the bottom half is filled with bursting energy.

The intrusion of people is diminished with the tiny tent on the edge of the picture, suggesting that we are merely guests of nature. Interestingly, there are no people in this photo. Every feature in the lower half of the frame contributes to the endless story of interplay of wind, waves and rocks in nature on the shores of Lake Superior.

Bill was never comfortable with dropping the overt Christian message, but he knew that alienating big chunks of his audience would never accomplish anything. He changed the title of his slide show from *God's Grandeur* to *The Timeless Wilderness*, developing a reputation in Winnipeg as a wilderness photographer and inspirational speaker, not an evangelist. Bill learned that as an artist, not as a zealot, he could make contributions to protecting nature by capturing its beauty and sharing his art. As a result, he reasoned, people would be more inclined to see the wilderness as something to be cherished rather than conquered. As hopelessly naive as this may sound, this was exactly how his life's work unfolded.

It wasn't until his last film, *Waterwalker*, that Bill ever brought up the subject of Christian faith in one of his films. Interestingly enough, in *Waterwalker* there are more references to aboriginal tenets of faith than to Christian ones.

From this modest beginning Bill became a great influence for environmental protection in Canada through his films, books and paintings.

Some of Bill's best still photography was completed on early canoe trips with Don Campbell, providing a great training ground for his later work in motion pictures. His trusty Rolleiflex was a basic camera, demanding a good knowledge of lighting, exposure and composition to get the right results. Since there were no automatic settings, Bill was in charge of every decision. Just the fact that the camera had no zoom lens meant that much more attention and work were required to get perfect framing. He shot slides, not prints, so cropping in the lab to make better compositions was not an option. What Bill showed in his slide show was exactly what he saw through the camera's viewfinder. Anyone who has shot stills with a good zoom lens, and then changed to a fixed focal length lens, has probably been surprised at how difficult it is to find the right position to get the perfect composition.

It is difficult to say precisely what made Bill's images so powerful. However, his sense of composition was one of his strongest assets.

"In our culture it is really tough to talk about spiritual things . . . you know the feeling . . . oh, oh, here comes the sermon. And no matter what I say . . . I can't win . . . because my church crowd will feel I didn't say enough and my canoe cronies will say, 'Well, we enjoyed the picture, but we really could have done without the sermon.' So what are you going to do?"

"I look around me at the colours, the textures, the designs. It's like being in an art gallery… God is the artist and he's given us the ability to enjoy all this and to wonder, and in our own small way to express ourselves through our own creativity… and that's why I like being here."

Bill Mason, Waterwalker

The subtle theme in Bill's slide show, The Timeless Wilderness, *is our diminutive presence in nature's grand scale. The composition of this shot, taken on the cliffs of the Barron River in Algonquin Park, shows the tiny figure at right as observer of nature.*

Using the camera's eye: composition, colour, perspective

All of Bill's films and paintings carried his signature style: powerful compositions and dramatic lighting conditions.

The strong diagonal line bisecting the picture adds drama to the already stark contrast between the evening sky and the silhouetted camper. Notice that there is "nothing" to the right of the guy-wire—the emptiness tells the story of the camper, alone, in the beauty of nature, in this case Lake of the Woods.

"It's really tough . . . I mean finding a way to make a living out here. For years I didn't even try . . . I was working as a commercial artist. And every spring I would quit my job to roam around from breakup to freezeup, and sometimes I would take along a friend, or I'd work as a guide at a children's camp (Manitoba Pioneer Camp). And I really enjoyed showing people what I had found out here . . . And gradually painting and photography became a way of sharing my experiences with a much wider audience. I prefer painting but film is just about the next best thing to taking you with me. The problem with film . . . if you show it the way it really is, everybody goes off to sleep . . . stories, films and legends have portrayed wilderness as a dangerous place to be . . ."

Bill Mason, Waterwalker

The Georgian Bay pine, swept by wind into a permanent lean to the east, is made even more dramatic by the stark black silhouette on the blue and pink sky. This shot looks deceptively simple, but it required a careful set-up to be sure that the sun set behind the trees at the right spot. Bill probably camped on the same site the day before, studying where the sun set. There is also a narrow window of time to capture a sunset, as the sun goes down fast once it reaches the horizon.

Silhouettes and back lighting

Bill, inspired by the painter Tom Thomson, experimented with black silhouettes in this photograph to capture the feeling of deep forests. The trick is to expose for the sunlit trees in the background (i.e. reduce the aperture, allowing the foreground to be underexposed). Once again man is relatively small and not the subject in the picture, merely an observer. Bill created silhouettes by shooting in natural light, without flashes. Today's automatic fill-flashes, even on the smallest and cheapest cameras, would expose these silhouetted trees, losing the drama in this photo.

Northern River *(1917)*
by Tom Thomson.

Composition: extreme framing

By dropping the treeline and blazing sun to the bottom one-tenth of the picture frame, Bill created an impression of infinite, amorphous clouds. Composition like this is important in capturing the grandeur, majesty and scale of wilderness.

Lightning: a difficult subject

Anyone who has tried to capture lightning on film has experienced the frustration of ending up with a roll of black photographs. It is almost impossible to anticipate where lightning will strike, let alone react fast enough to release the shutter. You also need nerve to stand outside in a lightning storm with your tripod firmly grounded in the rock, inviting the lightning to take the shortest route to Mother Earth . . . through the tripod's metal legs. Add to this the discomfort of getting soaking wet, and you have a tough photographic assignment.

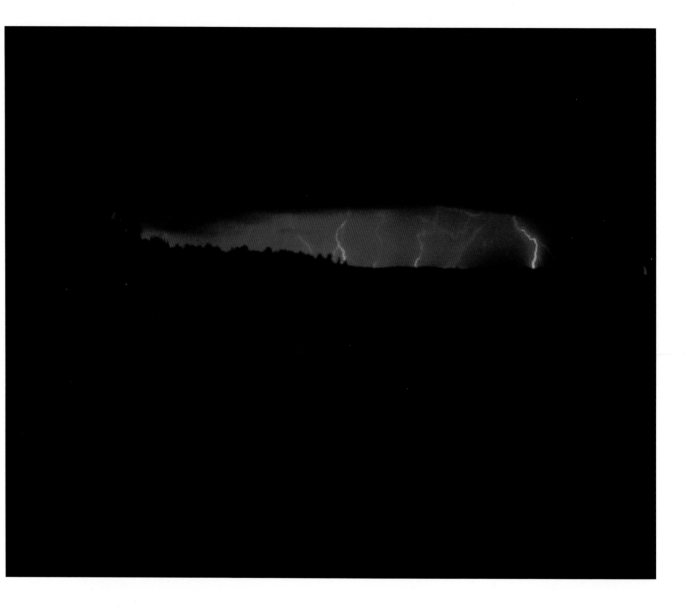

The classic clichés

"Never ignore the clichés because people love them," was one of Bill's maxims. He always had the audience in mind when shooting stills or films, knowing that if he gave them beautiful images then he could also promote environmental responsibility.

Shooting calendar photographs

Because Bill often paddled alone, he was more attentive to the details for a perfect composition, becoming a master at setting up campsite shots. Both these shots are classic examples of perspective and balance, making the scenes feel appealing, idealistic, and even romantic.

ABOVE Every detail has been considered—the canoe and paddle have been carefully placed. The fact that the top of Bill's head is just below the waterline in the background is not a happy accident; if he were positioned a little higher, the shot would not be as effective.

RIGHT Again Bill used the silhouette, exposing for the water and sky and allowing the foreground to go black. These camping shots, especially useful for calendars, were used in his commercial art contracts.

It's not camping; it's living outdoors

When Bill made people the subject of his wilderness photographs, he showed them in comfortable harmony with their surroundings. He regarded wilderness as a sanctuary, not an adversary. Even his shots of running rapids had him in control, not on the edge. Bill took books on canoe trips, finding time to read every day. He also included his sketch pad, oil paints and cameras, all of which were means to connect with the beauty around him.

Bill made a distinction between "camping in the wilderness" and "living in the wilderness." He regarded every wilderness trip as the latter, with the difference being in the mind of the traveller. Just as an urban home offers refuge from the world, Bill felt that wilderness offered sanctuary from the world of cities, traffic, television, noise and pollution.

Home is where the Baker tent is (home is where the heart is)

Bill didn't want to romanticize life in the bush; he figured it was beautiful enough to speak for itself. Bill welcomed the rain as it gave him an excuse to laze around all day under the canopy of his tent by the campfire. The Baker tent, also called a campfire tent, was perfect for a day like this since heat is reflected from the campfire into the tent, much the same way as a reflector oven. Bill hosted fellow campers under his canopy when it rained—they couldn't stand up in their high-tech tents.

It got so warm inside his tent that it was possible to dry out wet clothing while it was still raining. The design, originally from Calvin Rutstrum's book, Paradise Below Zero, *published in 1946, evolved from simple lean-tos made from a single sheet of canvas.*

The Baker was also a perfect winter tent; the reflector wall behind the fire threw heat into the tent. Even though it was open on one side, the only tent better for winter camping was a walled canvas tent, complete with wood-burning stove. Bill pointed out in The Timeless Wilderness that living outdoors in any conditions can be done in comfort if you have the right equipment and attitude. "We are smart enough to live outdoors," he explained. "We just have to make up our minds to work at it."

Canoe studies: a lifelong project

Bill meant it when he declared: "The canoe is the most beautiful thing ever made by man." He took every opportunity to photograph the canoe and some of his most successful paintings were those in which a canoe was the subject. And, of course, almost every film he made had a canoe in it. Even his ad campaigns for trucking companies had canoes in them.

An obsession with light

Bill tried to use light in his photography like a painter uses paint in a painting. Bill's hero, J.M.W. Turner, was radical in his depictions of light, spending a lifetime painting the sun. "The sun is God," declared Turner on his deathbed. It was reported that just as he died, on December 18, 1851 in his room overlooking the Thames River, a sudden shaft of brilliant winter sunlight flooded his Chelsea bedroom. Whether this story is apocryphal has not been determined, but it has become part of the Turner legend, and it caught Bill's imagination.

Taking a reading into the sun closes down the camera's aperture since a lot of intense light is coming through the lens, causing the shadows to go black. The little slice of light on the gunwale of the canoe (below left) gives the canoe dimension.

Experimentation with extreme lighting

Using a long exposure resulted in a soft focus on the water, complementing the overexposed moon.

Bill liked to shoot in low natural light. Instead of a flash he used a white reflector board to fill in shadows. He carried old newspapers, balling up the pages and throwing them on the fire for a brief but intense light. The dark blue sky in this shot suggests that the sun had just gone down behind the horizon, leaving just enough ambient light in the background. The camera, mounted on a tripod, was activated by a remote device, usually a long string. It was easy to feel that all was right with the world when camping with Bill.

"I'm really afraid that people are losing the ability to actually see the world around them. I like to think that my films encourage people to see the world around them with new eyes. We look at things but without insight and thought. If we would just slow down and synthesize the information that we see with our eyes, how could we not care about the natural world?"

Bill Mason, The Genial Fanatic, Man Alive, CBC

Remote firing devices

Bill travelled solo in his early years, so he had a problem if he wanted to take his own picture. But he was ingenious in setting up remote shutter release mechanisms, such as this one from the canoe. The point of this photo is to show how he set up shots of himself and started the camera from a distance. The stick, with the string and weight, was part of the firing mechanism that he activated by pulling a fishing line that ran under the water to the canoe. Many of the shots in The Timeless Wilderness *included similar set-ups. The black camera on the tripod is Bill's trusty old Kodak 16 mm CinéSpecial, which still works fifty years after he bought it.*

Seeing through new eyes

Bill used the camera to show people familiar things, but he did it in such a way it was as if they were seeing them for the first time, yet knowing them differently. This was equally true for the spider web as fragile microcosm and the wilderness as delicate macrocosm.

CHAPTER 5

ANIMATION

In the studio at
Meech Lake

If you want an animation stand, build one

BELOW Bill, Tony Peters and Tom Glynn checking out animation for The Wizard of Oz *at Crawley Studios in Ottawa.*

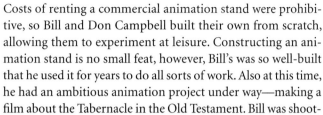

Costs of renting a commercial animation stand were prohibitive, so Bill and Don Campbell built their own from scratch, allowing them to experiment at leisure. Constructing an animation stand is no small feat, however, Bill's was so well-built that he used it for years to do all sorts of work. Also at this time, he had an ambitious animation project under way—making a film about the Tabernacle in the Old Testament. Bill was shooting tabletop animation using clay figures, but he also shot cell animation using his stand. He borrowed a Kodak CinéSpecial 16 mm camera.

In 1958 Budge Crawley, of Crawley Films in Ottawa, hired Bill as an animator for *The Wizard of Oz* series. Crawley Films was known as one of Canada's most exciting and adventuresome film houses. Bill moved to Ottawa, took up residence in his tent at Meech Lake and began commuting to the studio. By this time he had already developed a reputation for being a wilderness photographer and filmmaker (*Wilderness Treasure*), environmentalist, and a hot property as a commercial artist. He had starred in Chris Chapman's film, *Quetico*. He was also ambitious: it was his all-consuming dream to make films like his mentors, the documentary filmmakers Grant Crabtree and Chris Chapman. In addition, he was determined to transform Holling C. Holling's classic children's book, *Paddle-to-the-Sea,* into film.

Bill's work for Budge Crawley was a major step in his career as a filmmaker, leading to animation contracts with the National Film Board. Eventually these jobs resulted in a contract for his first NFB project, *Paddle to the Sea.*

ABOVE Bill working on some tabletop animation. He felt that animated Disney films were masterpieces, making a point of going to the latest one just to marvel at the drawings and artistic design. He often went to the movies, in the days before VCRs and DVDs, more than once so he could study the animation closely. He took Becky and Paul, of course, but to Bill Disney's movies were definitely not just kids' films—they were amazing works of art and storytelling for all ages.

LEFT Bill shot professional quality animation on his homemade animation stand, which could be easily disassembled and moved. For years it was set up in his parents' basement. On the table here is one of the backdrops for Tabernacle.

"There was a time when I was just fascinated with the history of the voyageurs. I read that stuff and I imagined that I was a voyageur paddling across the country and carrying hundreds of pounds of furs and trade goods . . . I dreamed about retracing all the voyageur routes and then I gradually became aware of what that era did to the native people . . . and I began to listen to what the great Indian orators have tried to tell us for over a hundred years . . . and we never listened."

Bill Mason,
Waterwalker

Bill's romantic perception of the voyageurs became tempered by the reality of how the fur trade negatively affected the aboriginal peoples' cultures. And by the '50s his admiration for these tough frontiersmen had changed to dismay with the destruction that the intrusion of European commerce and culture caused.

BELOW In this ad for Reimer Express, Bill used the voyageurs to make his point—the egotism of the bourgeois is funny and serious at the same time. His inflated superiority reminds us of the arrogance and the presumptuousness of colonizers and exploiters who believed this undiscovered land was in need of European civilization.

LEFT In cell animation transparent sheets (cells) with different components of a scene were laid on top of one another. The missing canoe was on a second cell which was laid under this cell with the paddlers. A camera took two frames at a time, then the cells were changed to depict the next stage, and so on. Film went through the projector at 24 frames per second, creating the illusion of motion.

Animation in *Path of the Paddle*

Animation was expensive, but since Bill could do every step himself—from drawing to shooting—he used it in his films without worrying about breaking the budget. In *Rise and Fall of the Great Lakes*, for example, animation demonstrated how the glaciers covered North America and reshaped the land as they melted. He employed animation to explain tectonic plates and volcanoes in *Face of the Earth*, while in *Path of the Paddle*, it helped illustrate paddling techniques, showed how moving water flows, and dramatized the dangers of getting crushed between a rock and a canoe full of water in rapids.

RIGHT This illustrates how water moves over rocks in rapids. Bill took as much trouble in painting his animated film scenes as he did applying oils to canvas. Painting on glass was especially effective to depict water and clouds. Bill used several layers of drawings to build up the image of the water. The layers of glass were stacked one on the other and then lit from an angle so light could "creep" between the layers, creating transparency and intensity of colour at the same time. These were animated only in the sense that they were shot on the animation stand as stills and then overlapped in mixes in the lab to show the changes.

BELOW It hurts to get caught between a rock and a hard place i.e., a canoe filled with water.

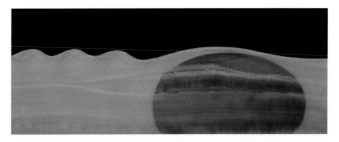

Animating maps: a lifelong passion

Maps fascinated Bill. He loved poring over them, imagining the many trips that he could do. Bill treasured a particular gift—a bound collection of topographical maps of all the canoe trips he had ever taken—given to him by friends. All kinds of maps, which adorned his studio walls, played a large part in many of his films. He was in his glory when making *Rise and Fall of the Great Lakes* since he had an excuse to actually animate maps depicting how the lakes were formed by the coming and going of the ice ages. He even animated the landscape in cross-sections, showing how the weight of the glaciers depressed the land and then allowed it to spring up again after they melted.

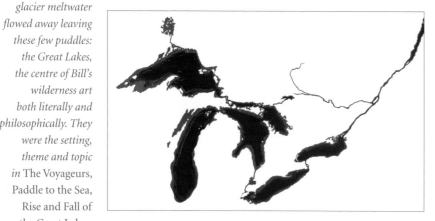

This was the second-last step in an animated sequence depicting how the glacier meltwater flowed away leaving these few puddles: the Great Lakes, the centre of Bill's wilderness art both literally and philosophically. They were the setting, theme and topic in The Voyageurs, Paddle to the Sea, Rise and Fall of the Great Lakes, Path of the Paddle, Song of the Paddle, Waterwalker, Where the Buoys Are, Coming Back Alive *and* Pukaskwa National Park.

"I spend a lot of time looking at maps. I plan some of my trips years in advance . . . and what I watch out for is where the contour lines all crowd together along the river and where the lines cross you can be pretty sure that the scenery is going to be spectacular."

—*Bill Mason,* Waterwalker

Animation in *Death of a Legend*

Bill had a serious point to make in his animation in *Death of a Legend*. He felt that Hollywood was doing a disservice to children who watched Disney's cartoon wolves, reinforcing misperceptions about the real animal as well as perpetuating and encouraging a belief in the legendary cruelty and blood lust of the fearful beast.

Part of his goal in *Death of a Legend* was to challenge people to set aside preconceived biases. While he conceded that there was nothing beautiful, charming or endearing about a pack of wolves worrying an animal to death, he accepted that they were just fulfilling their necessary role in the balance of nature. He challenged people to see this for themselves and to think critically.

Bill was torn between his admiration of Disney's animation as art and its exploitative depiction of nature. Bill parodied Disney's version of Little Red Riding Hood in *Death of a Legend*. The original fairy tale was based on the wolf as a predator dangerous to humans, but in Disney's hands the wolf was also a villain.

In a scene in Disney's *Beauty and the Beast,* for instance, the wolves chase Belle's father through the dark and scary forest as he narrowly escapes the snapping jaws by taking refuge behind the gate of the Beast's castle. The wolves, enraged at losing their kill, slather through the bars of the gates in great closeups, great that is if you don't mind being scared to death, never mind what's happening to your kids.

Preliminary sketches for the wolf animation in Death of a Legend.

SEQUENCE AT TOP The cells with the wolf's face were merged with the cells of the wolf's arm and the frightened pig to make the action complete. A background of forest completed the shot.

LEFT A stack of seven cells showing the wolf's arm reach out to snag the fleeing pig.

Don Campbell, a longtime friend of Bill Mason, helps set up a shot for the animated film, Tabernacle. The film was shot as a combination of tabletop and cell animation. It was the only time that Bill overtly discussed the subject of religion in any of his films, except for his last, Waterwalker.

The Tabernacle animation project

Bill worked on *Tabernacle,* an animated film that attempted to explain the role of the Tabernacle and the Ark of the Covenant in the Old Testament, for five years while at the University of Manitoba and employed at Phillips, Gutkin & Associates. To shoot the film, done with no financial support, Bill borrowed an old 16 mm Kodak CinéSpecial from Henry Reimer.

In his parents' spare bedroom, Bill built a huge diorama of the Israeli desert, complete with nomadic tribes and an oasis, all of Plasticine. He also built a walled city and, within it, the Tabernacle.

Perhaps the most effective shot was a zoom from a distant point, across the desert, past the shepherds and up to the walls of the city, through the gates to the steps of the Tabernacle. To start, Bill laid down track from an electric model train set. He then built the diorama of the desert. The track, buried under sand, started off-screen and led across the desert to the Tabernacle. Next, Bill mounted his CinéSpecial on a toy flat-bed car, placed the car on the tracks and moved it forward an eighth of an inch, shooting two frames. He cleared the tracks of some sand, advanced the car another eighth of an inch and shot two frames, etc. The zoom shot continued into the Tabernacle. The interiors were shot using cell animation.

Animated zoom shot from the desert to the Ark of the Covenant at the heart of the Tabernacle

The camera zooms across the desert to the city walls and then through the gates to the white walls and steps of the synagogue . . .

The camera continues the zoom up the stairs towards the burning altar and blue-curtained inner sanctum in which the Torah scrolls are kept in the holy ark . . .

. . . and as the camera approaches, the blue curtains are drawn apart by an invisible hand, revealing the holy golden inner sanctum and the ark, which contains the tablets with the ten commandments, the rod of Aaron and manna.

Backgrounds for Tabernacle. *Water colour on heavy paper board. Approximately 20" x 30". Circa 1955.*

Dragon Castle: tabletop animation

Santa brought Becky and Paul a huge box of Plasticine on December 25, 1977. Christmas day turned out to be one endless session of making things, anything, with the soft modelling clay. Bill, of course, was having as much fun as the kids. Little did anyone know that this would evolve into a new film idea, *Dragon Castle*. Becky and Paul took on the project, including

tabletop claymation, with Bill's guidance. The film was produced and put into distribution in 1980. It was, and still is, a favourite with children.

Bill and Becky arrange stills of the Dragon Castle *set.*

In many ways Dragon Castle *was a continuation of* Tabernacle, *with both using tabletop animation, clay figures and long zoom shots into rooms. Both films teach how we should define ourselves in the universe.*

CHAPTER 6

CARTOONING

Seeing life through the eyes of a cartoonist

Bill often vented his frustrations by skewering someone, or something, in a cartoon. He expressed his ideas, frustrations and affections far better in a cartoon than in words. His self-portraits captured a kind of self-deprecating humour, and at the same time, expressed warmth and kinship. Some of his most touching messages to friends and family were imparted in handmade greeting cards.

Bill's notebooks and sketchpads, as good as any diary, were filled with cartoon chronicles of daily events, expressing his thoughts and reactions to whatever came his way. And they were funny.

His cartoons revealed human foibles on a wide variety of subjects—from childrearing, pet care and gardening to canoeing and marriage. His cartooning might have been his least-known art form, but it provides the best insight into his personality.

One of Bill's favourite cartoonists was Charles M. Schultz, creator of *Peanuts* and a fellow hockey fanatic. Bill, who felt that *Peanuts* was a stroke of genius in its simplicity and penetrating look into human behaviour, was fascinated by the power that daily comic strips had to connect readers of all ages, emotionally engaging them in endless episodes. When he was involved with the wolf films, Bill called the alpha male Charlie Brown, perhaps giving Charlie Brown the upper hand just this once. Bill called the tamest wolf Sparky, Schultz's nickname.

In these postcards, sent to his children, Bill added a splash of humour, at his own expense. Canoe accidents were a recurring theme.

Postcards from a distant land

Whenever Bill travelled he sent postcards to Becky and Paul, but they weren't any off-the-rack cards. He drew wickedly funny caricatures of himself, often in scenes far from home where he didn't fit in. Cathartic when he was angry or frustrated, Bill's cartoons deflated pretension and ostentation.

Usually his cartoons expressed joy and happiness… and being alive. If anyone was being skewered, it was most often Bill Mason.

Self-portrait or happiness personified

LEFT Bill's own happiness was a frequent subject in his cartoons and this self-portrait, drawn after he retired from filmmaking to pursue his passion of painting, shows him in seventh heaven.

BELOW This was the notice that Bill circulated in the hockey locker room one morning to remind players to pay him for their ice time. As the financial wizard, Bill couldn't work miracles if they didn't pay up. He had glued a real one-dollar bill to the card, but of course, it was gone by the end of the game. Bill was the last guy who should have been in charge of the money, and he hated doing it. However, he wanted to play hockey so badly that he took on the job just to make sure that the games would go on uninterrupted.

Environmental issues

In Bill's mind one of the biggest threats to the environment was that all the great rivers would be harnessed and engineered to provide hydroelectric power—an attack on the lifeblood of wilderness.

Well aware of the benefits of hydroelectric power over fossil fuels and nuclear generation, Bill knew that supporters of hydroelectric power were turning a blind eye to their own problems. For instance, he said that the artificial lakes created behind dams were doomed to failure. They would fill up with silt; the recreational benefits in one place would be negated by losses in other places; the lakes were so big that they would create harmful microclimates; native fish stocks and whole ecosystems would die due to changed water levels and temperatures; megaprojects were more about political and national ego than about wise use of resources; lifespans of dams were grossly overestimated.

His main concern wasn't the fact that all the great canoeing rivers would disappear; it was our willingness to destroy rivers and their ecosystems in a futile attempt to feed our insatiable demands for power when alternatives were available and would eventually be implemented anyway. By then, however, the rivers would be lost forever. His answer was to develop other sources, such as wind and solar, coupled with conservation of power through personal actions.

Doodle, undated. Marker on paper (8-1/2" x 6").

Selfishness, shortsightedness and self-delusion are the themes in these two cartoons. Doodle, undated. Marker on paper (5-1/2" x 8-1/5").

Doodles, the telephone message pad

The Masons' telephone message pad was a sight to behold—sketches, caricatures, cartoons, anything but phone numbers and people's names. You had to wonder: What was Bill thinking about while listening on the phone? Did any messages get written down? Were the doodles reflections of what he thought about the speaker or about his reactions to what the speaker had to say?

From the message pad by the phone. Pencil, markers, etc. (undated).

A small sample of Bill's cards for his family over the years. While using himself as the butt of the joke, there was constant joy and love in his depiction of family life.

Greeting cards

It was a Mason family tradition to make cards for special occasions. And there was a lifelong running joke about Bill forgetting Joyce's birthday, their anniversary and other special occasions. While based somewhat on reality, the fact was Bill cherished these special days more than anyone, giving him an opportunity to make a new card.

Often the cards alluded to Bill's absentmindedness or to his outrageous gifts. One year Joyce's friend got a truckload of topsoil for her garden as a gift on Mother's Day. Joyce thought that this was a wonderful idea, especially since the topsoil at Meech Lake was thin and sparse. Consequently a load of topsoil became Joyce's perennial Mother's Day gift. Bill also bought her canoes (old and new), parkas . . . and a snowblower. Joyce, in turn, once bought Bill a lady's bicycle for his birthday.

As part of the family custom, Joyce made Bill an angel food cake for his birthday.

Much
Love
Bill.

HAPPY
BIRTHDAY
LOVE
Bill.

Bill's specialty were multi-panel cards where the front panel partially covered the inside panel with the first part of the message. The second part, often a joke, was revealed when the front panel was unfolded.

Many Happy Returns of THE DaY

The Return of Your
· Pairing knife
· Tape
· Pencil
· Scissors
· Calculator
· Touque
· Socks
· Mountain Bike
· Bucket
· Ruler
and may it make Your Birthday a HAPPY ONE

love. Bill.

MeRRY CHRISTMAS

TIle MASONS

YOU KNOW HOW IM NOT ALL THAT KEEN ON DRESSING UP......BUT

FOR YOUR BIRTHDAY IT'S WORTH IT

Much love Bill

When Paul married Judy Seaman in 1988, Bill and Joyce gave them a canoe as a wedding present. Bill made this card to accompany the gift.

Joyce's annual Mother's Day present of a load of topsoil for her garden.

One of Bill's earliest cards for Joyce. Bill and Joyce were engaged to be married, but Bill moved the Ottawa to work at Crawley Film Studios.

Awards and special occasions

My award for hitting the ball the farthest over the boards and into the woods.

This was how Bill announced that Path of the Paddle *had won a cash prize in a film festival in Oberhausen, Germany. He split the prize with me because I had shot the film and assisted in the editing. Bill always made a joke of his bad spelling by making up some outrageous attempt at the word.*

Bill made cards for the annual awards banquet to recognize everyone's special contributions to the Meech Lake Broomball Team, an unlikely collection of athletes, including Pierre and Margaret Trudeau, that played every Saturday night for years on the Mason rink. Bill had his own award: the Most Picked On Player.

CHAPTER 7

SKETCHES
& PAINTINGS

The sketchbooks

Bill always carried a sketchbook on canoe trips. Often he would slip away from the campsite for a while to sketch, creating beautiful images almost as if by magic. Bill's sketchbook, like most artists', was a private place where he experimented with ideas and techniques, free from scrutiny. The works were never meant to be finished pieces of art. Some were references for future paintings in the studio. Some were just a record of the trip, like a diary. Some were just for the glorious act of creating. Regardless, the privilege of looking through his private sketchbooks reveals a mind of many talents and interests.

Storm, Georgian Bay. *Oil pastels (4" x 2.5"). Date unknown.*

Following the masters

Bill's biggest influence in the art world was J.M.W. Turner, 1775 - 1851. Art historians classify Turner as a Romantic painter, often citing him as the father of impressionism in English painting, and one of its greatest and most prolific artists.

Part of Turner's appeal for Bill was how he rose out of the working class to tremendous success and controversy. The art establishment of the day could barely contain its outrage over his impressionistic style and, for some reason, often cited Turner's extravagant use of yellow as particularly offensive. Turner was rebellious in his art and flamboyant in his character. All this appealed to Bill.

Bill felt that studying the masters was one of the best ways to understand style, texture and composition. He scrutinized Turner's techniques with the palette knife and glazes for years. But most of all Bill was inspired by Turner's use of light. Turner was obsessed with light in his paintings. Bill was also a master at using light in his sketches, paintings and photography.

After Turner's Staffa, Fingal's Cave, *1832 (above). Oil on canvas (35.5" x 47"). Charcoal on paper (4" x 2.5"). Undated (circa 1984), sketchbook.*

After Turner's Snowstorm, *1842 (right). Oil on canvas (35.7" x 47.5"). Charcoal on paper (4" x 2.5"). Undated (circa 1984), sketchbook.*

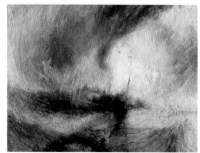

Bill had dozens of master drawings in his head that he could reproduce. He treasured the beauty of the master works, believing that they were the greatest resources that any serious artist could have. In a way he apprenticed himself to their creators. These studies were like conversations he was having with the artists, asking questions and seeking answers by following their hands.

Various studies from masters. Charcoal on paper (5.5" x 8.5"). Undated (circa 1982), sketchbook.

"I think it's good to have heroes . . . and mine is Joseph Mallord William Turner, a 19th century British master. When I look at a Turner painting, there's something about that guy— the way he captures a mood, or a feel(ing), whether it be a quiet morning, a thundering waterfall, or a raging storm—he just does it like no other artist I know. There's just some power there." —Bill Mason, Waterwalker

Life drawings

Untitled drawings from life class, circa 1980. Charcoal on newsprint.

Bill took life drawing classes all his adult life, on the theory that artists should be able to draw images of the human figure in its infinite manifestations. The results were startling in their variety and vision. As Bill moved away from film and back to painting in the early 1980s, he became more determined to return to the basics, keeping all his artistic expressions honest. While working on his films at the National Film Board, Bill honed his drawing skills by drawing thousands of images in his storyboards.

"Let sketches . . . be rapid, and the working of the limbs not too much finished. Content yourself with merely giving the positions of these limbs which you will then be able at your leisure to finish as you please."

Leonardo da Vinci

*Studies from life
drawing classes,
circa 1980 - 1986.
Charcoal on
newsprint.*

Untitled study of waves and light, circa 1978. Charcoal on paper (8" x 5").

From the sketchbooks: drawing the elements

Untitled, Nahanni River. Sketchbook #1, circa 1980. Charcoal on paper (8" x 5").

Untitled, circa 1984.
Charcoal (5" x 8").

Untitled, circa 1984.
Charcoal (5" x 8").

*Untitled, Georgian
Bay storm, circa 1980.
Charcoal (4" x 2.5").*

Untitled, lily swamp,
circa 1984. Charcoal
(5" x 8").

Untitled, Inuit dragging seal, circa 1960. Charcoal on newsprint (14" x 14").

From the Bill Mason sketchbooks, 1970 to 1984 (5.5" x 8.5"and 2.5" x 4").

*From the Bill Mason
sketchbooks, 1970 to
1988 (5.5" x 8.5").*

From the Bill Mason sketchbooks, 1970 to 1984 (5.5" x 8.5").

Untitled, Virginia Falls, Nahanni River, Northwest Territories, circa 1985. Charcoal on paper (10" x 16").

The sketchbooks:
painting in the field

In the early 1970s Bill decided to change his style of painting—to combine energetic impressionistic techniques and still have a narrative statement.

He began to experiment. He stopped using brushes, painting exclusively with a palette knife. The knife lacked the precision that he achieved with brushes, but the knife made the art more spontaneous. Bill gave up control for a more subtle and dynamic effect. It was not unusual for him to destroy pictures in progress because the knife was not cooperating, and the painting was, as he said, "turning to mud." When his palette knife technique worked, the results were spectacular. He could render the transcendent beauty of the natural world. And, while you can see the influence of Turner, there is no mistaking that Bill had his own style. They both shared a passion for expressing the intangibles of light, water and sky.

Perhaps Bill's spontaneity was at its best in the field. Like most artists, Bill did field paintings for reference back in the studio to paint a larger rendition. Two of his field painting sketchbooks are shown in the photograph at right. The small one is 4" by 2.5" and the other is 8.5" by 5.5". The pictures that follow are taken from these two sketchbooks unless otherwise noted.

Bill Mason, at his Meech Lake studio easel in 1980, was first a painter in heart, spirit and ambition. He felt that painting was the purist expression of his relationship with the land. While film was a more effective medium for reaching a large audience, showing Canadians their land as they had never seen it before, Bill could hardly wait to finally put down his camera and pick up his paints once more.

Photo by Becky Mason and Reid McLachlan.

Bill could achieve a remarkable degree of realism with the palette knife, yet the style remains imprecise, even coarse. The knife is a blunt instrument when it comes to including detail, but the detail is there.

Untitled, sketchbook, circa 1980. Oil on paper (7" x 5").

Studies of clouds

Untitled, sketchbook, circa 1980. Oil on paper (7" x 5").

The small paintings in this field book are quick studies where Bill experimented with dramatic colours and different layerings of paint with the palette knife.

Bill's technique of over-painting with the palette knife created moody images. The atmosphere here captures the approach of clouds and mist pouring over a mountain. Anyone who has travelled in the wilderness will recognize the inevitability of bad weather.

Untitled, sketchbook, circa 1980. Oil on paper (7" x 5").

Untitled, sketchbook, circa 1980. Oil on paper (7" x 5").

Untitled, sketchbook, circa 1980. Oil on paper (7" x 5").

Studies of the sun and sunlight

Untitled, sketchbook, circa 1980. Oil on paper (7" x 5").

Some of the results of Bill's experiments were quite startling. But knowing that his sketchbook was just that—a sketchbook that would not be scrutinized the same way as a final painting—he experimented at will.

Untitled, sketchbook,
circa 1980. Oil on
paper (7" x 5").

*Experimental sunset,
circa 1980. Oil on
paper (7" x 5").*

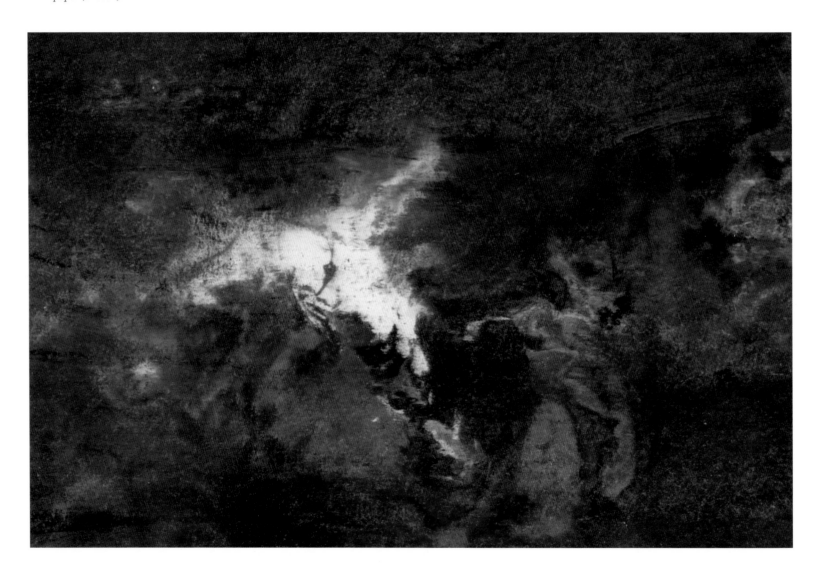

Untitled, sketchbook, circa 1980. Oil on paper (1.5" x 1.5").

Fascination with the power of water

Bill found beauty in water's wild energy. One of his biggest concerns was that all the great rapids and falls in Canada would be inundated and harnessed for hydropower—the thrill of approaching the maw of a canyon thundering with truly wild water could be lost. And once the dams and the generating stations are built, there would be no way of restoring the rivers to their natural state. His obsession with falling water explains why so many of his paintings capture the raw and elemental power of water.

Details from various paintings, circa 1985. Oil on paper.

NEXT PAGE
Details, Wilberforce Canyon, Northwest Territories, circa 1985. Oil on paper.

Detail, the power of water in a Lake Superior storm, circa 1984. Oil on Paper.

Details, the power of water, circa 1985. Oil on paper.

CHAPTER 8
THE STORYBOARDS

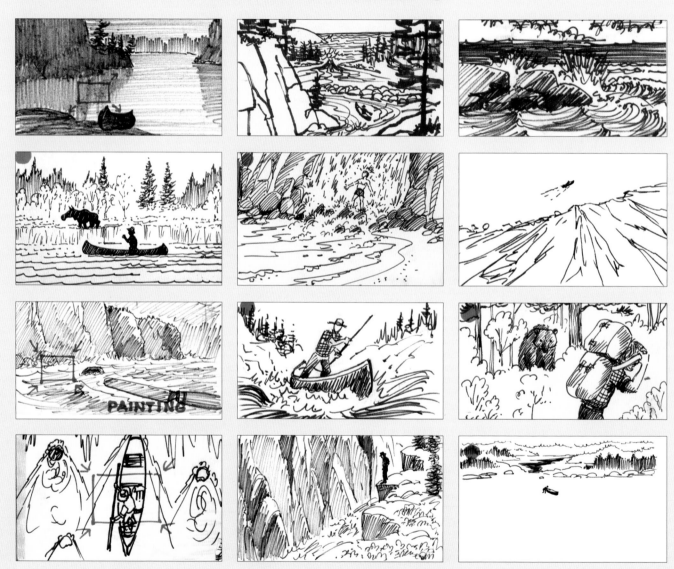

Dreaming through storyboards

It's obvious that Bill expressed himself most eloquently in images. It was natural then that he did most of his script writing in the form of pictures. His storyboards were always things of beauty, energy and vision.

The term "storyboard" comes from the cork bulletin boards found on the walls of producers' offices with attached sketches to illustrate an idea for a film. The whole film could be presented on the wall in a series of drawings on file cards. A storyboard looks a lot like a comic book, with the advantage that the pictures can be rearranged to help visualize shooting and editing the film into its final structure. The storyboard also has the decided advantage of being an inexpensive way to develop ideas for films.

You can also easily drop or add an idea just by taking it off or adding it to the board. Often the individual drawings have other instructions about music, sound effects and dialogue.

Storyboards are necessary in filmmaking since it is such a group effort. No other art form requires coordination of so many diverse artists, e.g., directors, electricians, picture and sound editors, photographers, stunt people, musicians, set designers, costume seamstresses, publicists and many others. The storyboard keeps everyone focused on what is being discussed by having a visual representation as each group adjusts its plans for the film.

Walt Disney used elaborate storyboards in the 1930s to plan his animated films. Because Disney started in animation, it was natural to draw an outline of the film to develop the idea, so it was an easy transition to use storyboards to develop live-action films.

When Bill went out on location, he taped all the individual pictures end-to-end, folding them together, accordion style, into a little booklet held together by an elastic band. He carried the whole film around in a shirt pocket. It was necessary to have the storyboard on location in order to keep the crew focused on getting all the necessary shots, angles and points of view.

Storyboard panels from the tracking up-river scene in Waterwalker. *The red dots indicate that the shot is done and "in the can."*

Storyboard panels from the dramatic downstream run at the conclusion of Waterwalker.

DOWN FROM TOP LEFT Magpie River; Little Thompson Rapids, Petawawa River; The Natch, Petawawa River; The Natch, Petawawa River; Rollaway, Petawawa River; Montreal River Canyon under the highway just north of Sault St. Marie, before the hydro dam was built; point of view, Montreal River Canyon; emptying canoe at the end of the run, Little Thompson Rapids, Petawawa River.

As he got the shots required for each sequence in the storyboard, Bill put a red dot in the top left-hand corner of each frame. It was satisfying to see the storyboard on the studio wall with an increasing number of red dots. However, some shots stubbornly refused to fall into line, remaining dotless. They were constant reminders of bad luck or bad planning.

In spite of repeated attempts, one frame in the storyboard that never got its red dot was a shot of the tent with lightning in the sky above and behind it. Bill knew it was possible because he had succeeded in the past in getting still photographs of lightning. Finally, Bill put a red dot on it after he had the lab insert lightning artificially.

Miniature masterpieces

Bill could spend hours drawing and revising the storyboards. His sketches varied from hurried minimalist outlines to beautiful renderings. But hurried or not, the drawings were dynamic and expressive, and obviously made with a passion for the subject matter and the act of drawing.

ABOVE *Sunset in* Path of the Paddle: Flat Water Solo.

When we were on long drives to locations, I drove the car while Bill mused over the storyboard. Many times not a word was spoken for well over an hour as he lost himself in his latest vision of the film. When he got a new idea, he quickly drew a new sequence for the film. Then we would talk about it. Often by the time we arrived at our destination, the film had changed dramatically. Bill couldn't resist going back to the storyboard after we got the shots to redraw individual panels so they resembled the actual shots very closely.

This was one of our most successful shots. It is so unusual to have the sun go down right into the water. Usually there are some clouds just at the horizon's edge, even on the clearest of evenings. We shot this from the foot of the cliffs on the south side of Old Woman Bay on Lake Superior. We used the 600-mm lens on the Beaulieu camera, mounting the camera and lens on a tripod in the water so they were only six inches above water level. The footing was treacherous on the slime-covered, rounded boulders. In order to get low enough to see through the viewfinder, I sat in the water. Bill helped me get set up and then raced out in the canoe to get into position. By the time he got back, and we had recovered the camera gear from the water, it was pitch black so we had to spend the night at the foot of the cliffs in rough terrain. We built a fire and dried out, enjoying one of my most memorable nights in the wilderness. The beautiful sunset, the monumental cliffs, the inland sea were so inspirational; the warmth of the fire, the luckiest guy in the world—what a job!

FAR LEFT *The power of the water is very clear in this simple little sketch as is the strength and skill required to guide the canoe downstream.*

LEFT *Just as the films were being made in the '70s, new technology made the Baker tent obsolete. The new high-tech tents, produced from computerized plans, were much more practical. This sketch shows a classic rendering of his beloved tent.*

The dream sequences (or, what fell onto the cutting room floor)

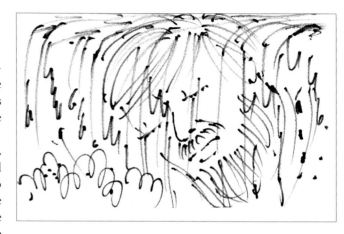

When Bill tried to get financing for his full-length feature documentary, *Waterwalker*, everyone he spoke to wanted to reshape the film to make it "more marketable." What they meant was that they wanted to rewrite the film, making it more attractive to mass audiences—to "Hollywoodize" it.

At first Bill was tempted to give in to their suggestions. After all, they were big-time producers who knew how to pull in the large audiences and large profits. They hectored Bill into self-doubt, but he wasn't worried about making money because he knew that by the time all the expenses had been paid there wouldn't be any money left anyway. He learned this when he made *Cry of the Wild*, his first feature documentary.

He was afraid, however, of making the most important statement in his life about wilderness . . . but nobody would see it. He was tempted to compromise with the moneymen: dramatize so people would pay to see the film, sacrificing valuable time that could be used for sharing his vision.

He considered taking a page out of *Rise and Fall of the Great Lakes*—use humour to entertain while getting across his message. There could be a level of satire pointing out the foibles and superficiality of Hollywood's culture, specifically the casting of the natural world as a dangerous adversary. Bill fantasized how he could take revenge on all the producers who would turn his film into a pseudo-adventure drama—man against the wilderness, a conflict complicated by "bad guys." Bill's plan was to use a series of dreams and daydreams, making his way through the wilderness in perfect control, safety and comfort.

Bill started drawing storyboard scenarios for these dream sequences, with the Hollywood hero in some sort of dangerous or dramatic situation only to escape through some dramatic or clever act. The idea was to end each dream sequence with a shot that shattered the Hollywood stereotype by having the hero do something bigger and more dangerous and impossible than any Hollywood hero had ever done.

One dream sequence made it into Waterwalker. *This storyboard panel shows Bill waking from a dream of the ultimate whitewater challenge—going over Niagara Falls in a canoe.*

Soon it became evident that this addition to *Waterwalker* was impossible. It would be far too expensive to shoot all the scenes without more money from the very people he was criticizing. It would also drastically change the tone of the film.

But an unexpected pleasure arose out of those storyboards. Bill could imagine taking on all of Hollywood, and winning. Paradoxically, Bill enjoyed Hollywood wilderness adventure films for their ability to hook an audience and to put them on their edge of their seats for the most preposterous reasons. He saw Hollywood films as engaging stories told by master storytellers. However, he resented having the wilderness depicted as a dangerous place, alien to ordinary people.

While the purpose of storyboards was to explore treatments of topics without the great expense of actually making them into a film, the simple truth was that Bill got a kick out of doing them.

The Airplane Gets Shot Down dream sequence

One suggestion was to have a plane wreck in a remote wilderness area, with Bill paddling wild rivers to safety. Presumably this explained why Bill was in the wilderness since no one would go there voluntarily, according to Hollywood logic.

Bill, minding his own business, inadvertently flies into unwelcome territory where a bad guy shoots him down . . .

. . . with the plane on fire, Bill desperately attempts to control it, but . . .

. . . he cannot gain altitude, so he cleverly guides the plane into the tops of trees which . . .

. . . cushion his crash landing . . .

. . . shaken, but not stirred . . . he disentangles himself from the wreckage and sets off to find his way home by canoe. He just has to make it back to civilization, but the bad guys want to finish him off so he won't report their illegal activities to . . . well, you get the idea.

The Indian Attack dream sequence

The Deadfall Trap dream sequence

The "wild Indian danger" stereotype is parodied in this dream sequence.

Even while portaging a canoe, Bill runs faster than the Indians.

By setting up ingenious traps, the enemy is relentless in attacking Bill.

A takeoff on Indiana Jones being chased by natives.

And finally, a parody of Butch Cassidy and the Sundance Kid when they jump off the cliff to escape their pursuers.

Logic is not a requisite in dream sequences, so Bill could wake up without solving the problem of what he was going to do with a canoe broken in two.

The Bear Trap dream sequence

In his attempt to make it back to civilization, Bill must be clever enough to overcome many dangers.

The comic touch in this sequence is that Bill can't open the bear trap because he isn't strong enough so . . .

. . . he carries it all the way home to show Joyce.

The obligatory *Deliverance* dream sequence

No Hollywood wilderness adventure would be complete without stereotypical neanderthal locals who beat you up just for perverse pleasure.

These dreams are the product of Bill's imagination, so why wouldn't he be the hero of his own dreams?

Bill escapes by being smarter than the thugs who are really the henchmen of the brains behind the conspiracy which made it necessary to shoot Bill down in the first place. . . . Well, you get the idea.

The *Jaws* dream sequence

As can be seen, Bill had a wonderful and unique perspective on the world. It is not hard to imagine these sequences, and the ones on previous pages, as animated films. The humour is typical of Bugs Bunny or Roadrunner gags.

The Jaws sequence is more over the top than the movie by having the shark bite the canoe in half, with Bill doing his "Waterrunner" trick of escaping by running so fast that he doesn't sink into Lake Superior.

The Wild Kingdom dream sequence

The scandalous revelation that Disney staged some of its Wild Kingdom footage enraged Bill. It turns out that the famous scene of thousands of lemmings hurling themselves into the sea in Alaska was staged with about 50 animals in Manitoba. Bill had no patience with filmmakers who passed off captive animals as wild ones. He felt such mendacity was professional dishonesty. In his wolf films, Bill studiously and overtly made it clear when he used captive wolves.

In this send-up Bill wanted to show the wildlife filmmaker arriving with a menagerie of caged animals, ready to provide any animal that the director might want. The scene got more and more ridiculous, concluding with the filmmaker producing an elephant and crocodile out of nowhere.

The Sudbury Smokestack dream sequence (or, what should have made it into the film)

The idea of satirizing Hollywood, and the ersatz culture that it encourages, was just too big and digressive to survive the final cut. Bill was glad to let the satire go, but he regretted not using the dream sequence format to promote some of his favourite targets of criticism—the heavy polluting industries that were deliberately, and within the law of the land, abusing the natural world. This dream reflects a very real frustration that he felt in speaking out against pollution and the impossibility of actually stopping it. Bill expressed a burden felt by environmentalists in the early '70s when it seemed that no one could do anything to protect the environment.

In one of Bill's unused sequences he plugs a giant smokestack. The square indicates a zoom into the tiny figure scaling the stack.

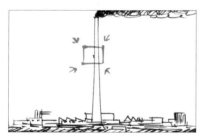

We would often see a yellow smudge of pollution from this smokestack miles away in the blue skies over Georgian Bay.

The scale of the struggle between the "little guy" and the giant industry stack is well represented in this aerial shot.

This sequence was to follow the pollution sequence filmed in the fume kill just northeast of Wawa, Ontario.

Because this was a dream, Bill could be unapologetic in its absurdity and simply cut back to reality.

The Marathon, Ontario Industrial and Sewage Effluence dream sequence

For 15 years Bill filmed pollution scenes in the bay outside of Marathon, Ontario. The pollution was unfailingly bad and spectacular. The affront committed against Lake Superior, and the environment in general, was disgusting. When we filmed there in 1976 we gagged on the fumes coming from the water and beach. It was all we could do to stay long enough to get the shots. We drove away quickly with the windows open, but we had a nagging feeling that we could never quite outrace the folly of mankind.

The polluted shores of Lake Superior in 1976. Acres of light brown foam, about seven inches high, float on the surface of the water, undulating like some cheap effect in a Hollywood horror film or a Government of Canada anti-smoking scare ad. Twelve years earlier, in 1964, Bill and

Blake James filmed a pollution sequence for Paddle to the Sea *at the same beach, in the same stench. Two years later they filmed a pollution sequence for* Rise and Fall of the Great Lakes *on the same beach.*

A sequence that did show up in the film (or, surviving a rogue wave)

There is a cachet about working in the wilderness. People think of it as being adventurous, perhaps even a little dangerous. Bill and I prided ourselves on having few misadventures, taking it as a sign of good planning. But Bill did upset and nearly drown on one occasion when we were shooting just north of Old Woman Bay on Lake Superior. He had not drawn a storyboard for this sequence, but he drew one after the fact.

Bill was paddling in big waves. From shore, I was picking off shots as the canoe climbed into the six-foot rollers. Since they were not breaking, Bill got more and more confident, going farther and farther in search of bigger waves. About one out of six waves was bigger than the others, and about the time he was over a shallow spot one of these rogue waves hit him. It flipped him into the water in a heartbeat.

This sequence is a good example of how the storyboard was redrawn after Bill capsized. We did not plan for Bill to just about drown in Lake Superior, but this accident was captured on film. Bill was playing in huge waves just off the northwest point of Old Woman Bay and I was filming the exciting action.

Bill abandoned his canoe, contrary to conventional wisdom, because the water was so cold. The canoe washed up to the beach about two hours later. If Bill had stayed with the canoe he would have succumbed to hypothermia.

He swam to a little cove in the rock face, but the backwash of the waves made it impossible to swim to shore. Fortunately the waves gave him a second chance by ebbing for a moment, then he managed to struggle to shore.

Bill was cold, exhausted and very shaken by this experience. We bundled him into dry clothes and sleeping bags. The next day we filled out the story by shooting closeups and low angles. We didn't shoot the recovery of the canoe that day since the lake was just too rough; we finally shot the recovery two years later. We were back at Old Woman Bay for another shot and running out of film. We only had 100 feet of film left, but the major shot was still not done. It was an exercise in shooting efficiency to get the shot completed with so little film. The hardest part was trying to bury the canoe in the sand so it looked like it had been washed up on shore and battered all day by huge waves. It's strange how we were reminded about the power of nature when trying to duplicate the simplest little thing.

Joyce, who was standing beside me, shouted, "He's over!" I was changing magazines at the time so a fresh 400-foot load was snapped into the camera—about twelve minutes of film. I focused on Bill with the telephoto, zooming out to get a good frame that included him and the shore where he would wash up. I figured that no matter what happened, I had better get this on film. If he survived and I didn't get the shot, he would kill me. But I had little hope that he would survive the cold water and the big waves—if one didn't get him the other would. I remember thinking that it was tragic that Joyce and the kids were going to watch him drown; we sent Becky back to the tent to get rope, a task that would take a long time. Joyce and I ran down to the cove where I tried to throw a rope to Bill. Usually I can throw a rope its own length, but this time the powerful onshore wind dumped the rope unceremoniously at my feet.

Photo by Bruce Litteljohn.

ABOVE *Bill canoeing the day after his capsize. Note the wave breaking in the background where he was flipped the day before. Occasionally even a small wave would break on the rocks beneath.*

Using storyboards in the field

These sketches from the storyboard represent shots in *Song of the Paddle,* the campsite at Old Woman Bay on Lake Superior. Often the sketches were used as inspiration for the sequence, but in this case they are akin to the final shot. Having the storyboard assembled like this was useful, forcing the crew to focus on specific tasks that had to be done. It was easy to be distracted by the endless possibility of shooting beautiful pick-up shots while postponing the more mundane but necessary shots.

FAR LEFT The actual scene through the camera viewfinder. Photo by Bruce Litteljohn.

LEFT The camera set up about 120 feet from the campsite. Photo by Bruce Litteljohn.

Sketches from the storyboard for the campsite shot at Old Woman Bay on Lake Superior.

When Bill and I talked about how shots were to be done, Bill often drew a sketch to explain what he thought the shot should look like. We discussed in great detail how to get the sketch translated to film, and once I got behind the camera and looked through the lens, the story would unfold.

Although these films and pictures were documentaries (not fiction or drama), they were carefully constructed. When Bill and I discussed a shot, we were trading variations on a truth until we merged our perspectives into a story that pleased us both. The shots told the truth.

In this sketch Bill is reading by candlelight until he falls asleep and dreams. The red lines represent compositions within the larger frame to zoom in and out. Fortunately this sketch was not compulsory, as we would need to set up the tent in the right spot, have proper lighting, a smoldering fire in the background, all the props, see if I could fit into the tent with the camera and tripod, and be prepared to solve any unexpected glitch.

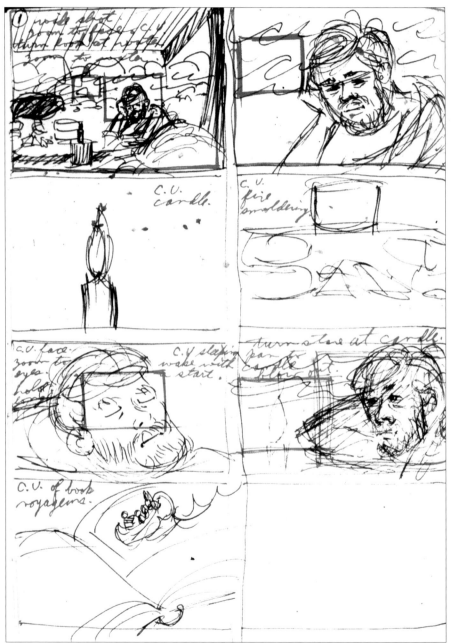

These pages from Bill's 8" by 5" sketchbook were the result of our discussions on what we were trying to capture on film. Bill drew them on one trip down the Petawawa River. Often we found an example of some hydrodynamics that would not photograph well, so we postponed getting that shot until we found a better location. Needless to say, this close analysis of moving water and canoeing skills was an opportunity to study the art of canoeing in minute detail. We also felt obligated to get it right because we knew that people would use these instructional films as guides on how to run whitewater, a potentially lethal activity if not done properly. We did these shots in about one week. Sometimes we returned to a location to pick up shots and solve problems we had found on the editing table. In those days before video, we never really knew how good the shooting was until long after we got home. We travelled down the Petawawa about 15 times.

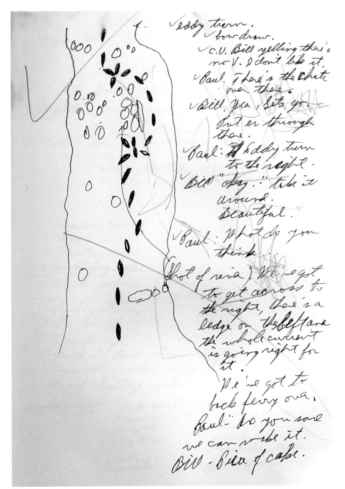

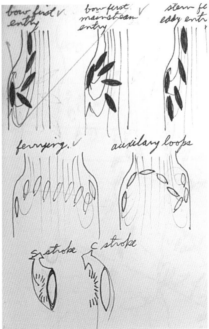

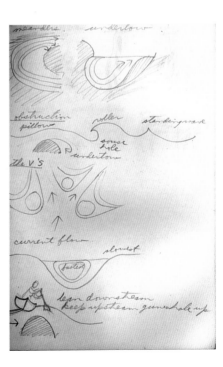

CHAPTER 9

FILMS

Quetico (1956)

Chris Chapman, one of the great Canadian documentary film-makers of the postwar years, had a contract in 1956 to make a film about Quetico Provincial Park in northwest Ontario. Later, in the 1960s, he went on to make the film *A Place to Stand* for the Ontario pavilion at Expo 67, winning an Oscar in 1968 for Best Short Subject. Ironically, one of the films he was competing against was Bill's *Paddle to the Sea*.

Shoal Lake

Chris needed a capable outdoors person to assist him in making *Quetico*. He had heard about Bill, mostly through Bill's slide show *The Timeless Wilderness*. He hired Bill as a guide, cook, portager and general gofer; but of course, the best part of the job was being the canoeist/actor for the film.

When Chris met Bill in Winnipeg to interview him for the job, Bill had just come back from a long canoe trip so he looked a little grizzled. Five months later, when the shooting finally began in late-August 1956, Bill thought that if he was going to be in a film he should shave and get a haircut. Imagine Chris's dismay when he met Bill at the train station to start their trip. Bill wore a hat through the whole film to hide his neat, citified appearance.

YEAR	FILM TITLE
1956	*Quetico*
1959 - 62	*Wilderness Treasure*
1963	*The Voyageurs*
1962 - 64	*Paddle to the Sea*
1965 - 66	*Rise and Fall of the Great Lakes*
1967	*Blake*
1968	*Death of a Legend*
1971	*Wolf Pack*
1968 - 71	*Cry of the Wild*
1974	*In Search of the Bowhead Whale*
1975	*Face of the Earth*
1972 - 76	*Path of the Paddle Series*
1972 - 76	*Song of the Paddle*
1980	*Coming Back Alive*
1981	*Pukaskwa National Park*
1981	*Where the Buoys Are*
1984	*The Land that Devours Ships*
1984	*Waterwalker*

Wilderness Treasure (1959 - 1962)

Wilderness Treasure was Bill's first motion picture, contracted by Inter-Varsity Christian Fellowship to make a promotional film about their summer camps. As a one-man production crew, the endeavour was a major learning experience, taking Bill four years to complete. But it was a good way to learn the film business.

The film is an extension of what Bill taught at Manitoba Pioneer Camp as a counsellor—travelling in the wilderness can be challenging, but you can do so comfortably; the wilderness is not an adversary which can't be trusted. He resisted the notion that people need to go into the wilderness to prove their toughness. That was missing the point.

The Voyageurs (1963)

Bill was hired as an expert wilderness guide, paddler and second camera in 1963 for a National Film Board project about the voyageurs. This was an experience that changed him forever, working with men who actually made their livelihoods in the wilderness as lumberjacks, fishermen and trappers. Bill was quite different from everyone else in the crew. He set up his tent out on points of land where there was a breeze and a view. The professional woodsmen thought he was crazy, pitching their tents back in the shelter of the trees. For this idiosyncrasy Bill was nicknamed the "Seagull." It didn't help either that Bill disliked beer.

An incident during this shoot proved to Bill how difficult it was to reconcile different attitudes about environmental responsibility. One night, camped on a beautiful island in Georgian Bay, the crew drank several cases of beer, smashing the empties on rocks. That night Bill warned the director that he was not leaving the campsite until every piece of glass was picked up, pointing out that he and his family would be camping at this very spot for years to come and he did not want to camp in broken glass. The next morning the hungover crew grudgingly picked up the glass. Thinking that was enough, they attempted to leave the bottles and broken glass in cardboard boxes at the campsite. They had to haul it all out, or Bill would not leave.

Bill often told this story to illustrate how people see the natural world differently. These men made their living in the wilderness, but they could see nothing wrong about leaving trash on a pristine site. Over the years Bill often pointed out that city dwellers, who merely visited the wilderness, usually felt a more compelling obligation to protect it, pitting the city tree-huggers against those who make their living in the wilderness. It's almost like they spoke different languages.

Georgian Bay

PADDLE TO THE SEA (1964)

Paddle-to-the-Sea: Holling C. Holling's children's masterpiece

One of Bill's great dreams was to make a film of Holling C. Holling's classic children's book, *Paddle-to-the-Sea*. Bill wrote scenarios, scripts and proposals for the film, trying to sell the idea to several backers. Bill was working on contract in 1963 for the National Film Board of Canada as an animator and cameraman. This gave him the opportunity to pitch his idea to the NFB, which finally bought it.

The storyline was a good fit for Bill; it was as if he had been training all his life to make this film—an odyssey made by a little toy canoe and its impassive canoeist, Paddle. A boy from Lake Nipigon carves a canoe, releasing it into the spring breakup so it can travel the waterways of the Great Lakes to the sea—a journey that the boy can only dream about. Children reading the book gain a new understanding of the Great Lakes by following Paddle on his journey. The story adapted well to film, providing a perfect vehicle for Bill's growing interest in environmental protection.

Blake James, who was also working as an animator for the NFB, was a partner in the project. These two friends set out on an adventure unequalled even by Paddle's journey. They travelled the Great Lakes for two years shooting the film as Paddle is swept through rapids, beset by curious animals, entertained by fireworks, almost dredged into oblivion, nearly burned in a forest fire and smothered by pollution. Paddle is also swept over Niagara Falls.

The film was nominated for an Academy Award Oscar in 1968 for Best Short Film, losing to Chris Chapman's *A Place to Stand*. The success of *Paddle to the Sea* firmly established Bill as one of Canada's foremost filmmakers. For many years the film was borrowed from the NFB library more than any other film. Teachers used it in their classrooms, resulting in most Canadians, who went to school in the late 1960s, '70s and '80s, having seen the film several times. By the late '70s it was not unusual to see three or four of Bill's films in the top ten of films borrowed from the NFB.

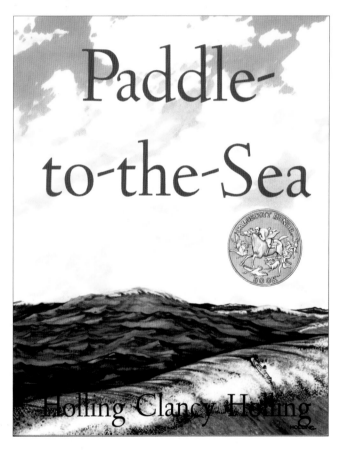

The cover of the children's classic story Paddle-to-the-Sea. *The film is faithful to Holling's original story.*

Courtesy the Houghton Mifflin Company.

On location: Lake Nipigon to the Atlantic

Bill and Blake searched out locations from Lake Superior to the Atlantic Ocean to tell the story of the Paddle's journey to the sea. They filmed every major geographical feature in one of the world's greatest watersheds, setting themselves almost impossible tasks and then taking great delight in accomplishing them.

They were gone for weeks at a time, living out of the back of a Land Rover. Bill stretched his budget as far as he could by avoiding motels and restaurants. They could both eat for about five dollars a day if they cooked their own food. And they could sleep for nothing in the tent or in the Land Rover.

By being a canoeist and an artist for a living, Bill made his dream come true. And his environmental stewardship took on new importance. Because so many children saw *Paddle to the Sea* at an early age, it was a great influence in shaping the imagination of Canadians about their own land. At that time it was one of the most powerful statements about environmental ethics made in film, and at the same time, it was subtle, gentle and loving.

Paddle to the Sea: the epic voyage begins

The story starts on Lake Nipigon in northern Ontario with a young boy dreaming of a far-away sea. During the long winter he carves the canoe with Paddle to the Sea etched on the bottom. The story tells the adventures that the little canoeist experiences as he makes his way to the Atlantic Ocean. Bill made many Paddles knowing that eventually some would be lost. Indeed, some were sacrificed to get the shot that he wanted.

The boy sets Paddle carefully, lovingly, and somewhat reluctantly, on the brink of a steep hill to wait for the approaching spring. Eventually spring arrives, the snow melts and Paddle slides down the hill into a swollen creek, launching his epic journey from Lake Nipigon to the Atlantic Ocean.

Paddle has many adventures and misadventures:
through big rapids, over dangerous waterfalls, getting snagged
on a fishing line, almost crunched by a laker in the Welland Canal
locks, frozen in ice over two winters, and almost abducted by a dog
and a little boy (three-year-old Paul Mason). Eventually Paddle
makes it down the St. Lawrence River to the Atlantic.

Shooting at Niagara Falls

One of the greatest shots in *Paddle to the Sea* shows Paddle going over Niagara Falls. Bill knew that if he asked for permission to climb over the restraining fences, to walk to the very brink, to float a waterproof camera over the falls in a home-made-raft made of plywood and an inner tube with a child's toy canoe attached to it, the authorities would emphatically say "No!" So, he didn't bother asking. He hoped that if he and Blake worked fast they could get the shot and then apologize for not thinking that they should ask permission. I never saw Bill look surreptitiously over his shoulder because he was doing something illegal, but perhaps this was the one occasion.

ABOVE
Bill prepares the floating camera to go over Niagara Falls.

RIGHT Bill, at the brink of Niagara Falls, filming Paddle as he goes over the falls.

ABOVE
Blake James rappels down to a vantage point. Blake and Bill went to any length to get a shot.

Paddle disappeared into the landscape on many occasions, which simply emphasized the scale of Canadian geography. The land is just as much a character in the film as Paddle.

OPPOSITE PAGE, TOP
Paddle at Devil's Chair Island, just off Cape Gargantua on Lake Superior.

RIGHT
Paddle goes over the big one, Niagara Falls.

OPPOSITE PAGE, BOTTOM
Paddle precariously perched on the brink of a falls in McCloskey Creek, Gatineau Park.

The floating waterproof camera: Magpie River in winter

Bill needed a waterproof housing for his Kodak CinéSpecial, so he manufactured one out of a recycled army surplus ammunition box. For a floating device to mount the waterproofed camera, he made one out of plywood and an inner tube. He delighted in fiddling with these devices, always improving their performance. He dubbed them "Mach I" and "Mach II" until he got to "Mach V," then he called everything after that "Mach V." He was particularly proud of the hockey stick attached to the bottom of the raft to hold Paddle in line with the camera—a very Canadian solution to a problem.

Preparing Paddle and the waterproofed camera above the falls on the Magpie River.

Paddle visits Manitoba Pioneer Camp

When one of the campers at Manitoba Pioneer Camp showed up with a snake, Bill filmed the snake visiting Paddle. Encouraged by this success, other campers showed up with frogs and a huge pike (still living). Bill got a great shot of a frog sitting on the little canoe with the pike lurking just below the surface of the water. Bill was also led to a pond where there was a semi-tame Canada goose, which cooperated on cue by checking out Paddle.

Paddle's journey to the sea

Bill could never pass on an opportunity to draw another map and animate a journey on it. He used layers of glass for the clouds to get a 3-D effect, employing these techniques in his commercial artwork for years.

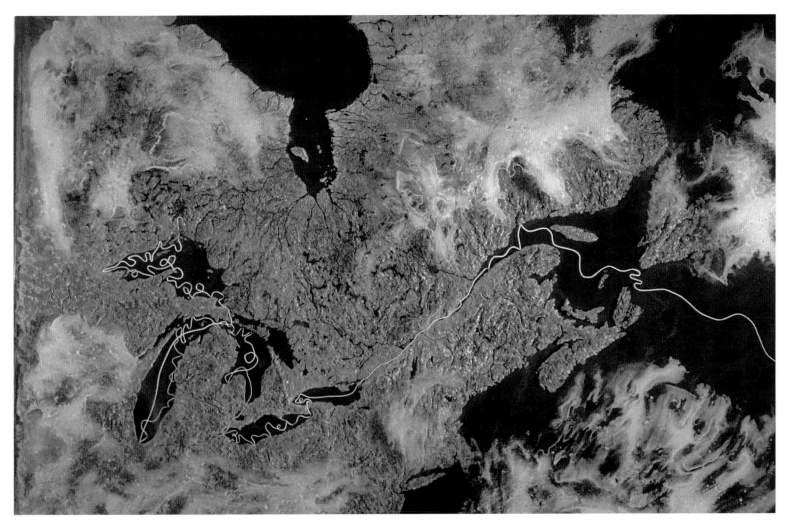

RISE AND FALL OF THE GREAT LAKES (1966)

Bill watches Blake put the finishing touches on Blake's double that was dropped from a helicopter into Meech Lake.

Canoes, glaciers and square dance music

Riding on the success of *Paddle to the Sea*, Bill was offered a contract by the National Film Board of Canada to make a film about the ice ages and the origins of the Great Lakes.

The idea was to have a canoeist who is paddling through the Great Lakes get caught in a series of time warps—bouncing back and forth in time. For example, the canoeist, played by Blake James, is ambushed by ice-age glaciers then instantaneously bounced to an earlier time when North America had a tropical climate, complete with crocodiles. The canoeist is helpless and hapless in such mighty changes of climate and geography. But he is also confronted by changes brought about by man, such as dams drying up rivers and pollution poisoning the water.

The grandiose title, *The Rise and Fall of the Great Lakes*, was chosen to complement the semi-serious events in the film. However the title was also meant to remind viewers that the very structures of the planet are in natural flux—through huge natural, even cosmic,

forces. But man is the first, and only, species to bring about changes as devastating as the shifting of polar locations and tectonic shifts.

The bounces in time, accompanied by square dance music composed by Bruce McKay, are directed by a square-dance caller who jauntily and merrily sends the canoeist on his wild adventures.

Blake James, the hapless canoeist in Rise and Fall of the Great Lakes, *paddling on Old Woman Bay, Lake Superior.*

Bouncing through time

The business of setting up the bounces through time required many steps. First, Bill and Blake needed two locations with enough similarities that they could pass for the same place—where Blake started and where he ended up after he got bounced.

For instance, they set up a tent for the first shot by taking a Polaroid picture of it. Then they checked out the second spot, using the Polaroid shot as a reference to be sure it looked like the first place, but with changes. Next, they went back to the original location to take the first shot. They kept meticulous records of everything, again using Polaroid shots, so they could set up the second location in precisely the same way as the first.

At the second location they re-enacted the action of the first scene using precisely the same camera angle and tripod height, lighting, costumes and props.

Blake starts at an idyllic campsite on Lake Superior back in a time when the land had not yet risen after the glaciers had melted. He is then bounced to the future and the water's edge is a hundred yards away. These are the Polaroid shots used for reference on location.

The two lower Polaroid shots were for shooting on the glaciers in the Columbia Icefields. While Blake is paddling he is bounced back to an ice age, atop a mile of ice.

This canoe trip lasts several ice ages

In one of the bounces through time, Blake is running a set of rapids which instantaneously dries up, making him crash into the dry rocks. He picks himself up, retrieves his hat and is shocked to see a huge concrete wall behind him. The river has been dammed, leaving him high and dry. Bill and Blake used the dam on the Montreal River for this shot in the film.

Blake is bounced to another time when the land is flooded, so he and all his gear float to the surface. This scene, shot at the foot of Dave Wright's dock on Meech Lake, was difficult to set up. All the gear was anchored underwater and then released on cue. Blake had to come to the surface at the same time as his gear. After many attempts and long hours in the water, they got it right.

Crash test dummy (dropping a canoeist out of the sky)

The most memorable bounce has Blake paddling along peacefully, minding his own business when suddenly the water freezes solid. Then the ice disappears causing him to fall about a mile into a swamp, where he has to escape crocodiles.

The real Blake could not survive such a stunt, of course, so Bill and Blake built a full-sized model of Blake in an old 16-foot canoe. They then suspended the canoe from the bottom of a helicopter and flew the prop to Meech Lake where it was dropped into the lake. There were three cameras shooting the event, but only the old pro, Grant Crabtree, caught the fall on film. Fortunately that was all Bill needed. With the key shot for the sequence completed, it was only a matter of filming Blake in the water right after the fall, cut in a marauding crocodile… and get a shot of Blake swimming for his life.

One of the cottagers at Meech Lake called the police about some crazy man being dropped out of the sky from a helicopter in a canoe. It was the kind of call that the duty officer probably still remembers and recounts as an entertaining event in his career.

Becky and Paul watch their dad make a model of Blake on the coffee table in their living room.

Bill and Blake had a lot of fun with the model, like driving around Ottawa with the dummy in the passenger seat of the car, or with the dummy sitting in the canoe tied to the top of the car.

On location at the Columbia Icefields

Bill and Blake travelled to the Columbia Icefields in Alberta to shoot a sequence of the arrival and departure of the glaciers for Rise and Fall of the Great Lakes.

TOP RIGHT
Acres and acres of foam floating on the water just outside Marathon, Ontario (1976). Bill used this location to film pollution scenes in Paddle to the Sea *(1963),* Rise and Fall of the Great Lakes *(1967) and* Waterwalker *(1976). The location was very dependable – it was always polluted.*

BOTTOM RIGHT
Shooting close-ups of Blake drinking the "polluted" water of Lake Superior. They used frothy hot chocolate.

The environmental message

Every film Bill made had an environmental message—some overt, some implied. The point was made directly in *Rise and Fall of the Great Lakes.*

It was accomplished with another bounce through time sequence. Blake, paddling in pristine water, scoops up some water taking a deep and satisfying drink of pure, cold water. His eyes wander to the sky as he scoops up a second cup, but now he has been bounced into the future—our time—to a bay on Lake Superior just outside Marathon, Ontario. The bay is covered in a light brown scum, about six inches thick. Blake isn't paying attention as he scoops up the scum and takes a big drink.

He explodes with disgust at the first taste of the "water," throws down his cup and quickly paddles out of the bay through scum that stretches as far as the eye can see.

BLAKE (1967)

Blake: the story of a man's passion for flying

Bill and Blake James worked on this project for over a year. This was the only film Bill shot in 35-mm; the larger format was more unwieldy than the lightweight 16-mm that he was accustomed to.

With no radio in the plane and all plans spelled out before Blake took off, the work was especially difficult. Any changes could only be made if Blake landed. Blake, notorious for getting lost, sometimes slipped into a reverie that came with flying, so he could be gone for hours at a time, leaving Bill feeling helpless on the ground. Blake, who controlled the cameras from the cockpit, flew around looking for interesting shots. He and Bill did shoot plane-to-plane, but even then all communications were made through the waving of hands and other gestures.

There were some great moments captured on film: Blake flying with Canada geese; Blake landing at Dorval International Airport in Montreal; Blake losing his road map while navigating and then coming back to snatch it out of the air. The last scene in the film, Blake playing in the clouds of a glorious sunset, shot from Champlain Lookout in Gatineau Park, is pure magic. In 1969 - 70 *Blake* got a lot of exposure when it ran as the short film with the original M.A.S.H. movie. *Blake* was nominated for an Academy Award for Best Live Action Short Film in 1970.

Blake James, born on a farm in Beausejour, Manitoba, was a talented artist. He first met Bill in Winnipeg when they were both commercial artists. Their career paths crossed many times, becoming the best of friends. Like Bill, Blake worked as an animator at Crawley Film Studios and later at the National Film Board. He and Bill worked together on many film projects: *Paddle to the Sea, Wolf Pack, Death of a Legend, Cry of the Wild, Rise and Fall of the Great Lakes* and *Path of the Paddle.*

And like Bill, Blake lived in a log cabin at Meech Lake. During the winter he worked on his plane in his cabin by taking it apart and bringing parts into the cabin one piece at a time. Visitors, invited in for tea, would have to struggle around a wing undergoing some repair that was suspended from the ceiling in the living room. The wing might be in the cabin for months. And when it was fixed, he would take it out and bring in the fuselage or the motor.

Blake, a self-taught musician, played the guitar in a unique plaintive style. His music, sparse and filled with unexpected rhythms and turns, spoke of the land. Even his liveliest pieces had a hint of sadness, loneliness or isolation. Bill used Blake's music for the film Blake *and as background to his slide show* The Timeless Wilderness.

THE WOLF FILMS

Death of a Legend (1968)

Wolf Pack (1971)

Cry of the Wild (1973)

Turning point: 1967 - 1970

Until Bill started work on the wolf project he had toiled in relative anonymity. He was well-known by those in the filmmaking industry, but the general public knew his films better than the man behind them. The wolf films brought great changes to Bill's life and career. He was about to become a very recognizable public figure.

First, it was the wolf pack in his backyard. Bill persuaded the National Film Board, Canadian Wildlife Services, Gatineau Park authorities and his landlord, David Wright, that he needed to have wild wolves in an enclosure behind his house at Meech Lake. He required captive wolves to film closeups of the social interactions among the wolves over a long period of time. The presence of the wolf pack in Gatineau Park was not meant to be a secret, but neither was it meant to be common knowledge. The news and rumours of wolves could not be contained. Even Prime Minister Pierre Trudeau and Margaret Trudeau dropped by one day after they heard wolves howling while at the prime minister's summer residence at nearby Harrington Lake. Speculation about Bill Mason, the Gatineau Park wolfman, became the buzz of the National Capital area. The attention was a double-edged sword for Bill. He had a love-hate relationship with the limelight. Even though it ate up a lot of his professional and personal time, he was pragmatic about his new power to advocate environmental responsibility. A part of him enjoyed the public attention, and he was not above modest grandstanding.

Second, with *Cry of the Wild*, about his wolf pack and how he made the wolf films, Bill was now in front of the camera, not behind it. With the spectacularly successful North American theatrical release of that film, Bill Mason himself became a celebrity—a spokesperson for environmental causes, a provocateur, and as Pierre Trudeau described him, a genial fanatic. Before this time Bill had always enthusiastically agreed to speaking engagements, public screenings and appearances at public events. But after *Cry of the Wild* he was in a whole new league. His personal celebrity drew renewed attention to all his films and his environmental ethics. He was constantly interviewed on radio and television, even invited to dine with Queen Elizabeth and Prince Philip at 24 Sussex Drive.

Third, Bill had in the past expressed his environmental criticisms in the subtext of his films, but in *Cry of the Wild* and *Death of a Legend* his criticism was overt and undeniably logical. He had become a high-profile environmental activist. With Rachel Carson's *The Silent Spring*, published in 1962, still fresh in the people's minds, the time was ripe for someone like Bill and his films. It was becoming obvious that environmental activism was needed to control industry and government.

For instance, Larry Gosnell, another Canadian documentary filmmaker, made a landmark film, *Air of Death* (1967), which eventually inspired the creation of Pollution Probe in 1969, and ultimately put environmental issues on the public agenda. Canadians were ready to listen when someone challenged the authority of government regarding environmental issues.

In some ways Bill's appeal was difficult to understand. He was an unusual figure in his floppy hat, moccasins and toe rubbers, green corduroy pants, cotton Baker tent and wooden canoes. But these were the very things that endeared him to the public. When Bill made *Paddle to the Sea*, the wolf films and the bowhead whale film, he was giving the world an antidote to bewildering, often frightening, events.

They were tumultuous times throughout the world during 1967 to 1970. Political and cultural revolution and civil unrest were everywhere. The United States was self-destructing over the war in Vietnam. During this time Robert Kennedy and Martin Luther King Jr. were assassinated, 15,000 Americans died in Vietnam and President Lyndon B. Johnson dropped out of the presidential race after an unrelenting media criticism led by Walter Cronkite. The Russians invaded Czechoslovakia in events that came to be known as the Prague Spring, the beginning of the end of the Soviet empire. Students rioted in Moscow, Cairo, Mexico City, Tokyo and many American cities. Riots and violence marred the American Democratic Convention in Chicago. At the Summer Olympics in Mexico City, a woman lit the Olympic flame for the first time in history. A few days later, on the winner's podium three black American athletes raised their fists in a sign of solidarity with the Black Panthers. Meanwhile, the phenomenon of Woodstock offered a powerful image to the world of America's hippie counter-culture of drugs, sex and rock 'n' roll. On the flip side, demented cult followers of Charles Manson murdered Sharon Tate in a psychopathic expression of revolution against the establishment.

We Canadians had just celebrated our centennial by hosting the world's fair, Expo '67 in Montreal, and we were still basking in the glow of its success. We were going to host the 1976 Olympic Summer Games. Trudeaumania heralded in a young, hip, charismatic leader who seemed to offer a brave new world of a "Just Society" in which, for example, the nation would remain united and bilingual. But the dark spectre of separatism tempered the optimism, and in October 1970 bloody civil unrest struck Canada when members of the FLQ (Front de Liberation du Quebec) kidnapped British Trade Commissioner James Cross and Quebec Labour Minister Pierre Laporte. Cross was later released but Laporte was murdered, with his body stuffed into the trunk of a car. Trudeau invoked the War Measures Act, jailing hundreds of people in Quebec without issuing warrants or laying charges. The FLQ criminals responsible for the kidnappings and murder were allowed to flee to Cuba.

Onto this world stage entered an "aw shucks" woodsman-philosopher, Bill Mason. He offered a reprieve from these worldly woes, providing Canadians a grounding in their heritage, their roots and their wilderness.

The wolf films: iconoclasm, the gloves are off

The wolf film project marked a turning point that changed everything for Bill. The Canadian Wildlife Services (CWS) wanted to commission the National Film Board to make a film about wolves, even seriously considering hiring a Disney crew.

But Bill's remarkable track record made him a hot property in the world of Canadian documentary filmmaking. He had just completed a series of hits, *Paddle to the Sea, Blake, Rise and Fall of the Great Lakes* and *In Search of the Bowhead Whale,* becoming the unofficial in-house wilderness filmmaker at the NFB. Two academy award nominations boosted his reputation. (The fact that Bill had just about died from a heart attack in 1964, and a year later, had been hospitalized because malabsorption problems had reduced his weight to 100 pounds, did not seem to dampen Bill's manic work ethic.) The NFB offered Bill the project.

Bill had never even seen a wolf in the wild, never managed such a huge budget and had no idea if he could actually make a successful documentary about wolves. But there was one thing about Bill: he was willing to be lucky, and he knew how to make his own luck. So he dove into the biggest project of his life.

The CWS and NFB had no idea what a wild ride Bill was about to take them on. Bill's title, *Death of a Legend,* summarized how the film changed from a Disneyesque pseudo-scientific story of wolves to an iconoclastic revelation of colossal mismanagement of wilderness and the environment. *Death of a Legend* used the plight of the wolf to illustrate our society's failure to appreciate the complexities of ecosystems.

Even Bill had no idea where this film would end up, but as he researched wolf behaviour he discovered a new world. He had read Farley Mowat's *Never Cry Wolf*, however, he didn't want to simply render Mowat's story, nor his interpretations about wolf behaviour, into cinema. So Bill went to the scientific community to get the hard science story. What he found, especially in the research by Dr. Douglas Pimlott, made it impossible to make a Disney story about wolves. For the first time in his life Bill jumped into politically hot issues. The most heated from the CWS point of view was that many Canadian jurisdictions had policies of controlling wolf populations through open-season hunts, bounty systems and poisoning programs using strychnine-laced baits. The film presented all of these activities as profoundly flawed in theory, purpose and practice. In reality Bill was not just targeting the CWS, but a systemic cultural bias against wolves in particular.

Years earlier, in 1956, when Chris Chapman and Bill were shooting *Quetico*, they spent many hours together talking as they canoed through Lake of the Woods. Chris, who was from Toronto, had big-city ideas that ran contrary to what Bill had learned; raised as a small-town boy in the narrow confines of working-class Winnipeg, he came to trust that the church and God could be invoked to make the world a better place and was encouraged to never question authority. Chapman introduced Bill to environmentalism as a political movement, pointing out that real environmental protection had to be won in the political arena and in the committee rooms. Bill understood exactly what Chris was saying but, until now, he always sidestepped the political side of environmental issues in his films. Finally, in *Death of a Legend,* Bill crossed the line.

Bill and Sparky in the wolf enclosure. Sparky, the lowest of the low in the social status of the pack, would shamelessly seek affection and interaction with Bill since she received no respect or friendship from any of the other wolves. Bill was definitely the alpha male in his relationship with Sparky. She would cower before him, squirming in submission at his feet, just as she would approaching the alpha male and female in the pack. But still she was wild. She was not a tame wolf, only a submissive one. She could be dangerous, but only out of fear, not out of aggression.

Death of a Legend (1968) and Wolf Pack (1971)

Bill was contracted by the National Film Board in 1967 to make two wolf films. One, a one-hour documentary about the scientific studies of wolves. Two, a 20-minute short to document the social interaction of a wolf pack. The first film, *Death of a Legend,* explained that healthy packs of wolves are not a danger, but a necessity, for healthy ecosystems. In the second film, *Wolf Pack*, Bill documented how wolf hierarchies are structured within a pack.

In *Death of a Legend* Bill pointed out that the "wanton killer" legend had its basis in truth, however, it has grown out of all proportion. Furthermore, the legend had enough strength to create a persistent—and lethal—cultural and legislative bias against the animal, making it acceptable to exterminate the wolf, and with the support of governments, we were well on our way to succeeding. He conceded that the animal is a predator, but showed that wolves do not kill wantonly. As part of nature, wolves kill to survive, usually hunting the weak and dying.

Bill wanted us to keep our legends in perspective. His thesis was consistent with his views on many other subjects as well. Bill was especially critical of the legends of intrepid European explorers "discovering" new continents where more than a million people already lived; the frontiersmen "taming the wilderness"; the missionaries introducing "heathens" to religion. He found it especially presumptuous for Europeans to rationalize colonizing other countries in the name of exporting "civilization" when they were really motivated by economic and political gains.

Once again Blake James teams up with Bill, this time for work on the wolf project. Blake, who plays the role of a trapper/hunter from the past for the sequence about the relationships between wolves and settlers of North America, helps manage the wolves while Bill is shooting.

Cry of the Wild (1971)

While completing his contract to make *Death of a Legend* and *Wolf Pack*, Bill became somewhat of a local legend himself. His reputation was growing as an important filmmaker. People had heard of his Oscar nominations and many had seen his films. But the rumours flew among the locals about a "wolf man" who had a pack of wild wolves in his backyard in Gatineau Park, only 20 minutes from Parliament Hill. Some people feared that wild wolves were being reintroduced to Gatineau Park, so their favourite picnic and beach spots would be in jeopardy.

The presence of the wolves helped fuel people's curiosity, but it became a problem. So many people made their way to the lake to drop in on the Masons, sometimes arriving at the most inopportune times, such as during filming.

Bill knew a good story when he saw one, and he realized that people were fascinated by his stories about working with wolves. Long before he had finished the two films, he decided to make a third one—a documentary about the making of the films. He had no budget to shoot footage for such a project, but he had so many out-takes from the first two films that it would not take much more shooting to round out the story. The NFB and CWS were definitely not interested in making a feature documentary about Bill and his wolves.

However, Ralph Ellis of KEG Productions was intrigued. Eventually Ralph partnered with the NFB and the U.S. distributor American National Enterprises to produce and distribute the film. *Cry of the Wild* grossed about $8 million, catapulting Bill from merely being one of Canada's most successful documentary filmmakers to one of the best-recognized environmental activists.

Used with permission of the National Film Board of Canada.

CRY
OF THE
WILD

"Cry of the Wild" is not just another film about wilderness. It is a dramatic saga about a man's search for the spirit of the wild in the most distant and remote areas of Canada's vast northland. For film maker Bill Mason, the wolf is the essence of wilderness, a symbol of all that is wild and free and untouched by man. To capture the wolf on film is to capture the spirit of the wild for all to share. Travelling alone and unarmed among wolves, Bill Mason has brought to the screen the life of the wolf and the world he lives in as it has never been filmed before.

The wolf films: the Meech Lake enclosure and managing wild wolves in the backyard

TOP RIGHT

Bill in the corridor part of the kennel with Charlie Brown, the alpha male, and Sparky, the lowliest female in the pack. These were the only two wolves that interacted with humans. The others were terrified if a human came too close.

It soon became obvious after preliminary research that most of the information about wolf behaviour would have to be shot in an enclosure. It was impossible to get close enough to free-roaming wild wolves to photograph anything in detail. Besides, that kind of wolf film had been made before.

The CWS, NFB and Bill agreed that the best place for the enclosure would be in Bill's backyard. His landlord, friend and neighbour Dave Wright agreed and in the summer of 1968 Bill had an eight-foot-high Frost fence installed, forming an enclosure about 150 feet square. Another fence was buried two feet deep at the base of the primary fence to stop the wolves from tunnelling their own great escape.

Bill hired friend and neighbour Cam Hubbs to weld an ingenious set of kennels that were tucked into one corner of the enclosure. A series of individual kennels, doors and a corridor enabled Bill to control which wolves were in the enclosure. The animals were rewarded when they were finally persuaded, or tricked, to go into the kennel. With the alpha male, Charlie Brown, in the kennel, Bill could persuade the lower ranked wolves to interact differently. This enabled Bill, to a certain extent, to control their behaviour. Usually there were only four or five wolves in the enclosure. But after a litter of pups was born, there were as many as 12.

MIDDLE RIGHT

Charlie Brown loved to have his stomach scratched. The safest way to do this was with a stick through the fence. When he had enough, Charlie Brown grabbed the stick faster than the eye could see. It was a stark reminder that this wolf could kill in three seconds if he wanted to.

When Bill was not filming, all the wolves were kept in the 150 square foot enclosure. Meanwhile local park wardens were busy delivering all the road kill that they could find in the park. In return, they had an excuse to drop by and visit Bill and the wolves.

BOTTOM RIGHT Bill could, and did, go into the enclosure to interact with Charlie Brown. If the big fella was in the mood, he allowed Bill to scratch his stomach as he lay on his back. But when he had enough he gave a deep growl. Bill knew that it was time to stop and leave—right away. Charlie Brown, who was as big as Bill, was definitely the alpha male in his relationship with Bill.

Shooting from platforms

Bill found it difficult to avoid getting the fence in his shots. There were two solutions: get height and shoot looking down, or try to shoot from ground level through the fence or even from within the enclosure.

Bill built a series of 20-foot-high platforms. It was cold business in the winter to be up on those platforms waiting for the wolves to cooperate. The blackflies in the spring were even worse. And when the leaves were on the trees, the platforms were useless.

Bill recruited willing volunteers to do things like throw bits of meat over the fence to get the wolves into position. But he also had the problem of getting to and from the platforms with all his gear. Sometimes he got the wolves interested in something at a far corner of the enclosure and then made a dash for the platform ladder. Unfortunately he couldn't come down until the wolves were lured away from the ladder.

It soon became obvious that all the wolves, except for Charlie Brown and Sparky, were more terrified of Bill than he was of them. Nonetheless, for the first couple of months, mostly at Joyce's insistence, a volunteer stood outside the enclosure with a .303 hunting rifle ready to save Bill from the wolves. There was never a need to use the gun. After a while Bill was more afraid of having an accident with the gun than being attacked, so he made a great fuss about taking the gun out to the enclosure to calm Joyce's fears, but he didn't tell her it was unloaded.

LEFT Bill on a platform while one of the low-status wolves feeds on a carcass that had been thrown into the enclosure after Bill had climbed the ladder. The fence and Bill's house are in the background. From the platforms, Bill got closeups of the wolves without getting the fence in the shots.

FAR LEFT Shooting in the spring. Once the leaves came out the platforms were useless.

LEFT Shooting with the 600-mm lens from a platform. This proved to be unsatisfactory because the slightest movement of the platform caused a gut-wrenching movement in the shot. The 600-mm lens had to be rock steady.

Two families—the Masons and the wolves

Much of the daily work required to keep a pack of wolves healthy and happy fell on Joyce's capable shoulders. Over the nearly three years that they kept wolves in their backyard, Joyce became quite an expert in managing their needs, especially their food. She did everything she could so Bill could work uninterrupted in the editing studio. Bill left her in charge for over a month on two occasions while he was shooting on location.

One of Bill and Joyce's great successes was the birth of a litter of cubs. It was probable that the alpha male and female would not mate in captivity because of no denning site. Bill made what he thought was a beautiful den in the middle of the enclosure, but the wolves rejected it, building their own.

The alpha female gave birth in the spring to five cubs. Bill built another den butted up to the fence. The back of the den was a removable plywood wall so Bill could film the birth of the cubs. Fortunately the female chose to use this birthing den and Bill got everything on film. He then closed up the back wall to leave the new mother in privacy, not wanting to make her so

The only wolf that Joyce trusted was Sparky who ingratiated herself to anyone who showed her any attention. Sparky could actually be a nuisance by getting in the way and fawning for attention. It was easy to think of her as a dog, forgetting she was wolf.

nervous that she wouldn't nurse. He was afraid that she might abandon the cubs, or worse yet, kill them because of human intrusion. But she seemed to be quite happy, enthusiastically taking on the role of mother. Soon after the birth she moved her cubs to the den she had built in the middle of the enclosure.

As an experiment, Bill and Joyce tried to acclimatize three of the cubs to human interaction. Bill got permission from the CWS to do this. The wolves were destined to always live in captivity, so it was not an entirely bad thing that they at least felt unthreatened by humans.

It was interesting that these three pups could never be trained or converted into domestic pets. They were hard-wired as wild animals and only thousands of years of domestication could ever take that out of their behaviour. They were never cuddly even though they were so cute—you just wanted to pick them up and hug them. But as soon as you did you felt an unrelenting resistance. They were squirmers, never getting the idea of snuggling on the lap of a friendly human being. Becky and Paul were so young that they could not really deal with the flailing claws and hyperactive activity. A close personal bonding between pups and kids just did not happen.

The cubs shortly after their eyes opened. Bill, who picked up shots at the mouth of the den using the 600-mm lens, refused to interfere in the life of the wolf family any more than necessary, especially while the cubs were young. This meant that he had to wait patiently for his shots and be ready when something happened naturally. It was impossible to predict what the wolves were going to do, and since they didn't do second takes, Bill had to shoot everything. The result was a very high ratio of film-shot-to-film-used in the final cuts.

The wolf cubs looked cuddly in pictures but they weren't. They were just not interested in interacting with humans. Even when drinking from a bottle they were constantly kneading with their sharp claws, making it almost impossible to cradle them. Below: Becky feeds one of the cubs. She wore long sleeves and pants to protect her from the cub's claws.

One of the cubs, still awkward on its feet when trying to negotiate the leaves and twigs on the spring ground, makes an adventurous foray out of the den.

Red in tooth and claw: survival

When the wolves first arrived at Meech Lake, there was great debate as to how dangerous they actually were. Bill knew, in theory, that the wolves should be so afraid of him that they would do anything to avoid him. But he also knew, in theory, that if they felt cornered they might fight because they couldn't run away from him like they could in the wild.

The raw struggle for supremacy within the pack was a study of pure power, red-in-tooth-and-claw. The postures and sounds that the wolves made in their normal interactions were truly primal, and very frightening. It was easy to understand the deep-seated visceral fear that we feel towards these animals. The growls and threats set off an involuntary fear reflex even in those of us safely outside the enclosure.

The wolves were masters of terrifying postures and sounds, but these were mostly bluffs and intimidation. It is not in a wolf's self-interest to fight with another wolf if intimidation will accomplish the same thing as a victory in a fight. However, if intimidation fails the wolf must fight, or submit to its rival's superiority. When the wolves bluffed humans, you could never tell whether they were really terrified or really angry. Nobody waited around long enough to call a bluff. After all, if the animal attacked out of fear, or aggression, the result would have been the same.

Bill and Blake take the wolf cubs on a canoe trip

Shooting in the enclosure was frustrating as it was difficult to persuade the wolves to act on cue, and often shots were ruined because the fence came into view. Then Bill had a good idea: he and Blake James would pack up the wolf cubs in travelling kennels and take them to 31 Mile Lake in the Gatineau Hills. They took the cubs to an island where they could run free and Bill could shoot without worrying about the fence. It was a good idea in theory: the cubs would be too scared to swim across the open water, so they couldn't make a break for freedom. The cubs were small and tame enough to be controlled, restrained, caught and put into travelling kennels, so Bill and Blake packed them up and headed out on a memorable camping trip.

The cubs were like three mischievous kids high on sugar. When they were released on the island they ran around like whirling dervishes, moving so fast that Bill couldn't get any useful shots.

Then more problems started to unfold. The pups were always hungry, naturally gravitating towards the food supplies. Bill didn't need shots of the cubs raiding the food box, but that's all the pups wanted to do. He couldn't even shoo them away; they would just play tag-team and sneak back when his back was turned. When the cubs had enough of this fun they ran away and hid. When Bill found them they were lying down, exhausted from their fun and games. Bill got a few good shots of them resting, however, watching the cubs sleep would not make for a good movie. After they rested they raided the food again.

Finally Bill and Blake had to concede that this shooting trip was a lot of fun for the cubs, but it wasn't going to get many shots for the film. They packed up and left. This created a whole new set of rules for the game of tag. Herding cats would be easy compared to cornering those cubs and returning them to their travelling kennels. After several hours, and using food as bribes and bait, they finally got the cubs under control and home again.

Bill and Blake constructed a catamaran by lashing two canoes together to ferry the cubs out to the island. Once there the cubs could run around freely but could not run away. Problems arose almost immediately when the cubs decided that they were hungry. They were always hungry, not grasping the idea that meals would be served according to Bill's timetable. They could smell all the goodies and wanted to eat them . . . now. Bill worried that the cubs, who were still wild but acclimatized to humans, would just run and hide. The opposite occurred—Bill couldn't get them out of the campsite to get a good natural shot. When they did leave it was to nap, which made cute pictures but of limited usefulness. Finally Bill gave up trying to get good shots and just let the cubs run around free until packing up for home.

On location in the Northwest Territories and Isle Royale

Bill travelled to the Arctic three times and once to Isle Royale, in Lake Superior, to film wild wolves. The Meech Lake enclosure was perfect for capturing detailed studies and analysis of wolf behaviour, however, Bill knew that the real story had to be told by filming wolves in the wild. Altogether Bill spent several months in the Arctic, sometimes in the company of others, but much of the time alone. He had no fear of isolation or the numbing cold. He was quite capable of surviving in comfort, preferring good igloos to a cold tent.

His real problem was trying to get the wolves on film. He was despairing that he would never see wolves in the wild, let alone get usable footage. He set up camp near kills, hoping that the wolves would return. He made blinds out of snow blocks, sitting in them for hours at a time waiting for the wolves to return.

The American equivalent to the Canadian Wildlife Service was conducting a groundbreaking study of wolves and their prey on Isle Royale in Lake Superior. While Isle Royale had no human habitation, it had a large population of moose. Wolves had been eradicated from the island in the early 1900s, but they had made their way back, establishing two or three packs. This was a good opportunity to study the relationship between wolf and prey. Bill was invited to go to the island to shoot film for his project, getting many good helicopter shots because the moose and the wolves had grown so accustomed to the noise of helicopters that they ignored them.

In the end the study disproved the legend that bloodthirsty wolves could, and would, wipe put entire populations of their prey. The study also proved that wolves killed only the weak moose in the herd, keeping the herd strong. It was a textbook example of the balance between predator and prey.

Getting ready for a helicopter shot on Isle Royale.

A shooting blind in the Northwest Territories near Fort Simpson.

On location in Ontario

Bill made several shorter shooting trips to locations in Ontario, most notably Algonquin Park where he met Ralph Bice, one of the original Algonquin Park guides and wardens. Ralph had always been a trapper and a hunter. He wrote several books about the history and management of Algonquin Park, and he was awarded the Order of Canada for his contributions to environmental awareness. He was informed and articulate, a perfect spokesperson for Canadians who actually live and work in the wilderness. Ralph and Bill had much in common in spite of their different backgrounds. They were both advocates for intelligent and constructive management of this country's natural resources. Bill accompanied Ralph on his trap line, filming the trapper at work. But the discussions they had about wilderness management proved to be as valuable as the footage. Ralph, who remained friends with Bill for years, offered insights that were a welcome counterbalance to the opinions and agendas of the scientists and urban environmentalists advising Bill. The result was that the films had a balanced and reasoned analysis of the wolf in nature.

IN SEARCH OF THE BOWHEAD WHALE (1974)

Bill's new high-profile reputation as an environmentalist, and his track record as an award-winning documentary filmmaker, brought him many offers to make films. He had just finished the wolf films in 1973 when he started his canoe film project. Even though he had an exhausting schedule, he couldn't turn down an opportunity to make a film for the World Wildlife Fund about the spring migration of the bowhead whale. Scientist Scott McVey and Dr. Joe MacInnis, Bill's friend, persuaded him to dedicate some time to work on the project. Bill set off quickly to Alaska to capture the study on film. They shot from helicopters and off the ice. Underwater photographers Joe MacInnis and Rick Mason (no relation) had the bone-chilling assignment to film the whales underwater. The film won many international awards.

Filming on arctic ice floes on the Beaufort Sea: fingers freeze to immobility, film becomes brittle and jams or even breaks in the camera, condensation forms on the inside and outside of the camera, delicate electric motors grind to a halt, batteries die in minutes. All in a day's work.

A bowhead whale, 70 tons of power, beauty and dignity, in the Beaufort Sea.

FACE OF THE EARTH (1975)

While making five instructional canoe films, Bill also made *Face of the Earth*, which illustrated Dr. Tuzo Wilson's theory of tectonic plates. The film has no people in it, just great examples of geological formations created by the inexorable forces of the floating plates and the unrelenting erosion by water. Bill used animation to illustrate the movement of the plates and formation of the earth's crust.

Larry Crosley's music score for the film is brilliant. The Canadian Brass plays Haydn's *Creation Theme* to represent the tectonic plates; Nexus creates sound effects for the underground pressures of magma; Eric Weissburg (Duelling Banjos, *Deliverance*) makes his banjo sound like water and erosion. This film is one of Bill's best, but it didn't receive the recognition that it deserved. It is worth watching just for the music, yet the combination of visuals and music is nothing less than inspiring—a celebration of natural grandeur.

THE CANOE FILMS

Song of the Paddle (1976)

Path of the Paddle (1976)

Waterwalker (1984)

SONG OF THE PADDLE (1976)

Song of the Paddle evolved out of the *Path of the Paddle* series. The one thing missing from the *Path of the Paddle* series was instruction on how to camp in the wilderness, or as Bill preferred to put it, how to live in the wilderness. There just wasn't enough time in the canoe instruction films to teach viewers about camping and canoeing skills, so Bill persuaded the National Film Board to expand the project to include a film on camping. The instruction is from a family canoe trip, with Bill, Joyce, Becky and Paul as the campers, of course. This film is whimsical and instructional, beautifully enhanced by Larry Crosley's score and David Campbell's songs.

Song of the Paddle: getting the family into the picture

One of the great things about shooting *Song of the Paddle* was that Bill and I had our families with us on location. Susan came along as a crew member and a still photographer. We had the best of all worlds—interesting work, clean air and water, wilderness and family.

Since we were teaching camping skills, we did much of the work at campsites. There we showed things as simple as making kitchen utensils and as subtle as considering wind direction when setting up a tent. We tried to adhere to the thesis that family wilderness camping should never be some sort of endurance test. Instead, we depicted camping as a simple, relaxing and enjoyable activity.

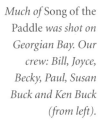

Much of Song of the Paddle *was shot on Georgian Bay. Our crew: Bill, Joyce, Becky, Paul, Susan Buck and Ken Buck (from left).*

ABOVE *Shooting a camp scene on Georgian Bay.*

LEFT *Susan, our still photographer on this trip, and me on location.*

Song of the Paddle: The Great Lakes

One of the most difficult questions we faced was where to shoot the film. We had a responsibility to the public to show safe canoeing. While wilderness travel has inherent dangers simply because you are isolated from emergency help, it is important to reduce the chance for accidents. For many reasons we chose Georgian Bay: the water is relatively warm, thousands of islands provide natural breakwaters for the waves that blow in from the west and the area is frequented by power boaters who could be approached for speedy evacuation. Today cell phones work in a large part of the French River area of Georgian Bay.

We filmed on one of the most dangerous of the Great Lakes, Lake Superior. Sudden big storms, cold water and no place to land because of cliffs presented many challenges. We purposefully filmed on realistic locations to teach the point that caution and safety are always paramount when canoeing, especially with children. The most important things to have are patience, time and extra food to allow you to wait for nature to give you a better day for travel.

ABOVE Creating confidence, the family plays in big waves near Byng Inlet in Georgian Bay when all four could fit into the 17-foot Grumman. They would start in a protected lee, go out into the waves and then back into the lee. We also had a second canoe acting as a back-up boat. In all our days of travelling in the wilderness with the family we never had one accident or even a close call.

RIGHT Lunch stop on one of the thousands of tiny islands in Georgian Bay near the Bustard Islands.

Song of the Paddle: campsites

Georgian Bay, after the kids had gone to bed.

Our job was to search for beauty through the eyes of a photographer. As we travelled through the wilderness we were required to be aware of the endless play of light, texture and composition of our surroundings. I developed what I call my "photography mode" of seeing, which is quite different from my everyday mode of seeing. It was necessary to turn off the photograph mode, even if just to rest my senses—it was like operating in high gear at full throttle. I still love throwing the switch into photograph mode just to appreciate reality in a different way. You don't even have to take the picture— just enjoy.

Georgian Bay—big sky, big water, big wind and thousands of islands.

ABOVE *French River, Joyce making early morning coffee.*

182

Song of the Paddle: running whitewater

Song of the Paddle was shot over a period of four years, so we were able to show how a family can make wise decisions while travelling in the woods regardless of the children's ages. Blue Chute on the French River was a great place to give the kids their first taste of whitewater. The rapids were Class I (the least difficult level) and safe. The water in the rapids was deep enough that if they did upset, neither the boat nor a person would hit a rock. And there was a deep pool at the foot of the rapids where we had a rescue canoe. Everyone wore the best life jackets. As the children got older, the family graduated to two canoes and increasingly more difficult rapids.

Bill and Becky run a chute on the Magnetawan River. We were constantly searching for locations where we could clearly illustrate a problem and the skills required to cope.

Blue Chute on the French River, 1970. The 17-foot aluminum Grumman was a perfect canoe for a young family.

Meech Creek in Gatineau Park. A simple excursion in a beautiful deep valley close to home.

Song of the Paddle: sailing

The sailing sequence was one of the most spectacular scenes in *Song of the Paddle*. We shot all day while Susan was busy taking stills. The sail was a quarter of a parachute, which we borrowed from Louise Brault, a neighbour at Meech Lake. We had planned for a single shot, but it evolved into a major sequence, celebrating freedom, sun and wind. We were still shooting at dusk when a sliver of a moon appeared on the horizon. We had just enough light left from the setting sun to light the canoe. I fixed the camera on the moon while Bill steered the catamaran between the moon and me. I pulled back to take in the whole canoe, panning it as it went by. We were sure that there was not enough light; fortunately, the shot turned out to be spectacular and one of my all-time favourites.

PATH OF THE PADDLE (1976)

Path of the Paddle is a series of four films, each 25 minutes long. They are some of the most successful films ever made at the National Film Board. Bill saw the project as an opportunity to take his viewers to some of the most beautiful wilderness in the Great Lakes region. It was said that these films contributed to the booming popularity of canoeing in the '70s and '80s. Bill's purpose was to show people that it was possible to live comfortably and safely on a wilderness canoe trip.

Bill needed a canoeing partner for *Path of the Paddle: Doubles Whitewater* and *Path of the Paddle: Doubles Flatwater*. Paul was a natural choice, being a good paddler. He had the added advantage of making the canoeing techniques look easy. Bill often joked about child labour and all the hardships Paul

endured—canoeing all summer, travelling in the wilderness, acting in films, staying in motels, eating in restaurants, sleeping in tents. We always invited one of Paul's friends—John Selwyn, Derek Brown or Robin Brown—to share his hardships.

In the end we realized that Paul was the only one who could have been Bill's partner just because of his availability; nobody else could have dropped everything whenever Bill needed to go shooting. Eventually Paul outgrew his plaid shirt during the four years of shooting. We couldn't find another one so Susan went to Toronto and bought Royal Stewart wool fabric to make a new one. For continuity the shirt had to lose its newness, so Susan washed the basement stairs with it, making it look exactly like the well-worn original.

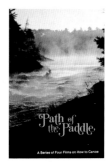

Used with permission of the National Film Board of Canada.

Picanoc River,
Quebec

Path of the Paddle: **Old Woman Bay, Lake Superior**

We shot most of the flat-water instructional sequences for *Path of the Paddle* on the south side of Old Woman Bay. It is relatively easy to get to and is spectacularly beautiful. You can see emerald-green castles of rock formations forty feet underwater. The 800-foot-high cliffs provided a shield from the sun, eliminating glare. At the base of the cliff we found a perfect shooting platform on a steep-sided rock that juts out of the water. We shot there for four consecutive summers.

Old Woman Bay meant so much to Bill that we scattered his ashes in the water at the foot of the cliff, just where we spent so many days filming.

RIGHT *Bill and Paul demonstrating a manoeuvre. The water in the foreground is about 20 feet deep.*

BELOW *Bill making his way down the coast of Lake Superior at the foot of the cliffs at Old Woman Bay.*

Our "shooting rock" was about 50 feet away from the base of the 700-foot-high cliff. The rock was about 15 feet high, with enough flat space on the top for three or four people to stand. While it was a comfortable platform for shooting, the sides were so steep that we had to use a rope to get up and down. We were constantly bringing camera equipment up or down so we didn't want to take any chances on slipping. This shot was taken from a canoe in the water.

To keep the lighting consistent we had to shoot the low angle shots facing the same way that we had shot the high angles—that is to say, with the sun behind us. Otherwise the high shots and low shots could not have been edited together. As well, shooting from such a low angle would provide a dramatic cutaway from the high shots taken on the shooting rock. This created a problem: there was no low-level rock on which to set up the camera. Luckily we found another rock, which lay about 20 inches under the surface of the water. There was just enough space for the tripod and me. The rock dropped off into about 20 feet of water on all sides, so I had to be careful. It was quite a trick to get to the rock and to set up. I was on this rock for hours, meaning I had to wear hip waders and heavy long johns because of the cold waters of Lake Superior. When I needed to reload, Bill would ferry film out to me.

WATERWALKER (1984)

Waterwalker is a 90-minute feature length documentary released in 1984. When Bill and I were working on *Path of the Paddle*, we always dreamed about doing a feature-length documentary about wilderness canoeing. The National Film Board was tempted, but wouldn't buy into the idea.

Bill had already had success with *Cry of the Wild* (1972), his first full-length documentary, which was basically made from all the out-takes from the wolf films. *Cry of the Wild* grossed about $8 million at the box office, a substantial return for a film that cost about $100,000 to make. Unfortunately almost all that money was eaten up through wrangling among American National Enterprise (the American distributor), KEG Productions (the Canadian distributor) and the National Film Board. Bill certainly did not see any of that money but he was hoping that he could repeat the success with a canoe documentary feature, and that maybe this time some of the profits would come his way.

A documentary feature was never far from our minds, so when we shot for the canoe project we would often do one more shot for the feature. We said this half in jest and half in earnest. But we knew that we could never do the shot more economically than at the time, so we accumulated a library of shots that could be used in *Path of the Paddle* but were actually better suited for a full-length documentary.

Finally the National Film Board partnered up with Imago, a non-profit organization. This was full circle for Bill in a sense because the director of Imago, Wilber Sutherland, was the same man who arranged the financing for Bill's first film, *Wilderness Treasure*, some 25 years earlier.

Alan Whatmough, a long-time friend, encouraged Bill to approach musician Bruce Cockburn about doing the music for *Waterwalker*. Cockburn wrote an original song for the film, collaborating with Toronto jazz musician Hugh Marsh to complete the score.

WATERWALKER
a canoe odyssey

a film by
Bill Mason
music by
Bruce Cockburn
& Hugh Marsh
cinematography by
Ken Buck

a National Film Board of Canada
and Imago co-production

DOLBY STEREO™
in selected theatres

Used with permission of the National Film Board of Canada.

Waterwalker: location, location, location

Panels from the storyboard depicting Bill's arrival on his upstream journey to Denison Falls. Black marker on paper (4" x 2.5").

Shooting the films *Path of the Paddle* and *Waterwalker* took Bill and me on very different adventures than the family film, *Song of the Paddle*. In *Waterwalker* Bill makes a journey upstream on an unidentified river to a watershed, and then portages to a new source and paddles back down to Lake Superior. The trip was edited together from a compilation of many locations, lakes and experiences. Reaching Denison Falls, a captivating water-falls, on the Dog River was one of the great landmark sequences in the film. We spent several days at this site capturing its power on film. Some of Bill's best sketches and paintings were inspired by this place. The falls are situated in such a way that for the most of the afternoon the scene is spectacularly backlit.

Waterwalker: **Cascade Falls, Lake Superior**

Cascades Falls, at the mouth of the Cascade River in Pukaskwa National Park, is one of the few falls that drops directly into Lake Superior. You can paddle directly to the falls from the lake. All the other rivers along the north shore have eroded their falls some distance upriver. Denison Falls, the last big drop of the Dog River, is found about a mile upstream from the lake. Bill first visited Cascade Falls in 1958 on his solo Lake Superior trip from Marathon to Michipicoten. One of the pictures in the Star Weekly article showed him having a shower in the falls. Sixteen years later we did the same shot in 16-mm for *Waterwalker*.

*Cascade Falls,
Lake Superior, 1974.*

Cascade Falls, Lake Superior, 1958. This picture appeared in the Star Weekly *in a special story on Bill's solo trip along the north shore.*

Taking a shower under Cascade Falls. It never occurred to us that the inviting sprinkle of water spraying over the falls would just about knock us down. Bill actually had to do a lot of acting to give the impression that this was a good idea. I switched from the Éclair on a tripod to the handheld waterproof Kodak CinéSpecial.

A sketch of Cascade Falls done on location. Sketchbook (8.5" x 6.5").

Panels from the Waterwalker storyboard.

OPPOSITE PAGE
Denison Falls, Dog River, late afternoon, 1984.

Bill is on a wilderness painting trip in *Waterwalker*. There is one scene that always elicits a collective gasp of dismay from the audience. Bill is painting the falls with his palette knife. His commentary explains that using a palette knife to apply oil paint to paper is an unpredictable technique, and that he would often give up to start a new painting. As he works on the painting, he sits back to look at it for a moment, evaluating it. He then picks it up, crumples it and puts it in the fire, obviously unsatisfied with the results. Most people in the audience would happily have hung it on their walls just as it was.

CHAPTER 10

BEHIND
THE SCENES

Camera equipment

We used the lightest camera equipment possible, contrary to the trend in the booming film industry that bigger is better, and coinciding perfectly with Bill's goal to capture undisturbed wilderness.

In order to be as unobtrusive as possible, we used only the smallest equipment, carrying it all in two Woods #1 canvas packs. The 16-mm Beaulieu camera was a beautiful little camera. We mounted the world's best lens on it—the 12-mm to 120-mm zoom Angenieux. We also had it adapted to take our Nikon lenses, especially the Nikon 24-mm wide angle, the Nikon 300-mm and the Nikon 600-mm. The camera took 100-foot (always measured in feet, not metres, for some reason) loads of film, which lasted about three minutes at 24 frames per second. The camera also had 200-foot magazines (so-called Mickey Mouse ears because of their shape), which were pre-loaded and changed quickly. They each lasted about six minutes.

It was not unusual for wilderness documentary filmmakers to hire powerboats, helicopters, planes, semi-trailer trucks and cranes to shoot a film. It was a trend that fed on newly available technology and, probably more likely, on big budgets. Some filmmakers helicoptered into a remote area, stayed for two or three days (sometimes only hours), got their shots and flew away. Television's growing appetite for programming created a market for such shows, and they did fill a growing niche. But Bill wasn't making films for TV; he was documenting the reality of wilderness, and to do that he had to be unobtrusive.

Bill and I talked for hours about what would end up in the final cut of our films. It was important to both of us that we accurately captured a truth. We were well aware of the privilege of working for the National Film Board of Canada, where we were not controlled by a profit motive or bottom line—we were free to get it right.

RIGHT The cascading water at Denison Falls on the Dog River. The cascading water has eight distinct steps. It is quite easy to climb up the rocks on either side of the falls in low water. But in high water the rush of water is monumental. The afternoon mist rising above the falls is back lit against the black wall of rock and trees.

LEFT The Beaulieu with a 200-foot magazine.

Using the Beaulieu camera with the Angenieux 12-mm to 120-mm lens with the tripod legs as low as they would go, with a 100-foot load inside the camera. We always used the tripod except when in the canoe. This extreme low angle resulted in a dramatic shot where the waves are actually higher than the camera. The shot to the right is typical of what I would see from this angle. Near Byng Inlet, Georgian Bay, 1972.

All documentary films are constructs born in the mind of their filmmakers. Even the most objective documentary film-maker is putting his perspective on the screen. Films are more like essays with theses rather than raw truth. Anyway, raw truth is often too boring, or too horrifying, to watch. To document (first used as a verb by Jeremy Bentham in the early 1800s) is a fairly modern term that arose out of the technical ability, and legal necessity, to literally create an official written record of legal standing of human activities.

The term documentary, when applied to film, usually means a story that is non-fiction. Still photographs are better than motion pictures at documenting something because they freeze reality in time. But even they are selected by the person who controls the camera, and photos can be cropped and used out of context. Today, anyone with a computer photo-editing program can alter images so they tell a different story.

Bill and I had several rules to enable us to capture the truth about wilderness. First, we had to be where the truth was happening—in the wilderness. Second, we had to disappear into the location so our presence did not change the wilderness. Oddly enough this is not as difficult as it seems.

My assignment was simple: go to the swamp at the end of Meech Lake and film wildlife activity for use as cutaways in the canoe films. I loved the idea of setting up a blind (like the real wildlife photographers) and hiding from the critters I was filming. One day I set up a crude, unobtrusive blind, copying duck blinds I had seen.

For several days I dutifully crawled into this blind and did my work, picking off beautiful closeups with a 600-mm lens. I came back one day to find that someone had destroyed the blind. While I was mulling over how to fix it, I just set up the camera on the edge of the swamp and stood there, very still. I let my mind wander into a meditative state. Time meant nothing.

I soon stopped meditating and started working because in a matter of 15 to 20 minutes the swamp decided to ignore me as it came to life. My discovery was simple: if you can remain absolutely still, wildlife will ignore you, and you can watch a wonderful world of nature unfold as if you are not even there. To this day I still like to do that trick. The most interesting part is how difficult it is to be absolutely motionless for 20 minutes.

Camera equipment: Beaulieu, Éclair, Arriflex

During the '60s and '70s the Beaulieu had a reputation among professional filmmakers as an amateur piece of equipment. They were wrong. For silent shooting (without recording sound) the camera was every bit as good as the Arriflex or Éclair, weighing about one-third of the bigger cameras. However, the Beaulieu was noisy so you couldn't shoot sound with it. When we shot with sound, we used the Arriflex and Éclair, with magazines for 200-foot and 400-foot loads that seemed to last forever. The Beaulieu had the added advantage of being light and compact, a major advantage when shooting in wilderness situations. All these cameras were battery driven, so we always carried at least three rechargeable batteries. The first thing we did when we got off location—even before showers and food—was to recharge the batteries. Dave Selwyn, our battery expert, was a big help keeping the finicky things going.

The Éclair with its 400-foot load. Being absolutely silent and with an extra long load, it was the Rolls-Royce of cameras.

The Arriflex with a 200-foot load.

Packing and carrying all that stuff

I liked to brag that I could carry enough equipment on my back in a Wood's #1 canvas canoe pack to shoot for one week. But there was another factor: we had to keep the gear dry. It is hard to believe today when there are so many good high-tech waterproof carriers on the market, but there was no such thing in those days. I exaggerate. Actually there was a good waterproof container called a plastic bag, and I suppose it could be considered high-tech when compared to waxed cotton bags. We wrapped everything—film, camera parts, lenses, still cameras—in its own plastic bag, sealed with duct tape. We then put each into larger plastic bags, sealing them with large elastic bands made from slicing car tire inner-tubes into one-inch strips. At any point in this process we liberally applied more duct tape. We put the big plastic bags into cotton bags to protect the plastic from punctures. We then put the cloth bags into a wicker wannigan. And finally, we placed the wannigan into a Wood's #1 canvas canoe pack.

I didn't have to carry all that stuff by myself all the time. On several shooting trips Barry Bryant signed up as a production assistant. Once, Barry kept track of the number of times he portaged the canoes back up Blue Chute on the French River while Bill and I were setting up for the next shot—21 times! Besides being as strong as an ox, Barry was a great cook. Those were wonderful times.

We never upset a canoe with a camera bag in it, but we came close on several occasions. Susan and I were paddling an 18-foot Grumman into Byng Inlet after shooting for a couple of weeks. The waves were pretty big and we were trying to paddle directly into the mouth of the inlet so we didn't have to contend with breaking waves on shore. We just happened to have all the camera gear and film in our canoe. As the waves began to break all around us, I did a quick calculation of how much all the stuff in our canoe was worth—about $120,000 in 1973 dollars. Needless to say, we took no chances then or any other day with our camera gear. But just the nature of our work meant that there was always the danger of losing all our stuff in a heartbeat.

The black changing bag

Loading film into the cameras was a task that could have catastrophic consequences if done incorrectly. When loading 16-mm cameras, you have to protect the film from any light. The black bag, a thick, light-proof cloth contraption, was used to protect the film. There were two ways that film was delivered from the factory. The first was daylight loads. These were metal reels that held either 100 or 200 feet of film. The reels had solid metal sides designed to protect the film from light so they could be loaded in full daylight. However, you always ran the risk of

Unpacking the camera gear on location, Old Woman Bay, Lake Superior. This plastic bag was our "high-tech" waterproofing system. Sometimes one pack contained more than $100,000 worth of cameras and film.

Fully loaded for a day's work on the Magnetawan River, 1975.

having light sneak into the reel and ruin the first, or last, 10 feet of film. This was a significant loss since the reels were only three minutes (100-foot loads) or six minutes long (200-foot loads). And, of course, you could ruin a once-in-a-lifetime-shot. As a result we used the black bag even to load the daylight loads. This black bag was pulled right over the camera and the cameraman, cinched at chest level—quite an unusual sight.

The second way film was delivered was on a yellow plastic core, with no protection from light by a solid-sided reel. This film was packaged in light-proof plastic bags, with no choice but to load and unload this film in absolute blackness. We used a different black bag, one with arm holes in it, so you didn't put your head in it to change the film, doing everything by touch inside the bag.

We couldn't always choose where we were going to change film while on location. We loaded/unloaded film in some of the most precarious situations. Cold weather made fingers clumsy when trying to persuade the film to slip into the gates and engage in the sprocket wheels. In warm weather I sweated profusely inside the black bag, sometimes onto the film and inner workings of the camera. I went under the black bag on the faces of cliffs, in the middle of rapids, in cars and planes, in parking lots, even in the bottom of a canoe tossed by huge waves. Passersby were attracted to the camera, having no hesitation about walking up to us and asking what we were doing. While the camera was a great icebreaker, when I went under the black bag people always walked the other way—it was just too weird.

My worst experience with the black bag occurred on Old Woman Bay, Lake Superior. We were shooting from a catamaran in calm water when the camera jammed. I had to go into the black bag to check it out. Rather than make the long trip back to shore, I tried to fix the camera in the canoe. The problem was more complex than I thought, so I was under the bag for about 10 minutes. By the time I came up for air I was seasick. The gentle rocking of the catamaran did me in. I was absolutely incapacitated. It was so bad that we paddled back to shore and drove 60 miles to a Sault Ste. Marie motel so I could recover. The good side of the story was that we got to see the

newly released film *Jaws* that night at the local theatre. I don't know if that helped my condition or not. It took three days before I was totally recovered.

When I think of the black bag, it seems so primitive. Video and DVD have changed that side of filmmaking today. There used to be a full-time person, the assistant cameraman, on big productions whose main task was loading and unloading films into magazines inside the black bags. Nowadays one person shooting videotape can do the job of a whole film crew.

This, I think, makes for better filmmaking, at least better documentary filmmaking. Now filmmakers are less hindered by the logistics and expenses that come with huge crews. They can get to places where important stories need to be told without an intimidating crew of technicians.

Bill and I tried to offer insights into the natural world not seen by the public. We tried to make films differently. Bill was a master at thumbing his nose at conventional wisdom about making movies, rejecting the idea that bigger is better. He always reduced the process of making film to the simplest common denominators: ideas, narrative and art.

Changing film under the black bag on the rim of Lady Evelyn Falls on the Sand River in Lake Superior Provincial Park. Even though I needed a safety rope on this location because the mist from the falls had made the footing on the rim treacherous, this was a routine change of film.

Special camera rigs and mounts: the catamaran

Bill setting up the catamaran in a sheltered cove. Old Woman Bay, Lake Superior.

Venturing out of the calm water in the cove into the big waves of Old Woman Bay. Bill, Bruce Litteljohn and me.

In the big waves at Old Woman Bay.

Ready to go.

The challenge when on location was to find the best way of capturing reality on film. To this end we developed several rigs and mounts. Some were made in a garage workshop, some were manufactured in a sophisticated machine shop. In those days the National Film Board had its own shop with technicians and engineers who created custom mounts and rigs for us. They worked perfectly as did our homemade units.

We often lashed two canoes together, using them as a catamaran to transport equipment or to provide a floating workspace. While the system worked well, the catamaran was difficult to manoeuver.

In this sequence we got our shots, but we were getting blown toward shore so I had to stop filming and help paddle. I really thought we were going to be washed up on shore. In desperation I leaned into the paddle, breaking it in two. Luckily we had a spare and we managed to work our way into the calm water of the cove. Bruce Litteljohn and Judith Dennison had joined us at Old Woman Bay, with Bruce helping paddle while Judith took stills.

The point-of-view shot: the helmet

The canoeist's point-of-view shot was difficult to get. Where do you put the camera? How do you hold a camera and paddle at the same time? Where does the cameraman sit?

For a skydiving film, the NFB camera department made a special device—a modified motorcycle helmet with a small camera on one side and a counterbalancing weight made of lead on the other side. The camera held 50-foot loads of 16-mm film, about 90 seconds of shooting. We got a few good shots with this camera, useful as cut-a-ways when editing the film.

Bill wanted a canoeist's point-of-view shot of upsetting in rapids and getting washed down in huge waves. We borrowed a waterproof camera from the camera department, mounted it on the helmet and counterbalanced it with the lead weight. I paddled Bill out to the top of a rapids, where he slid over the side of the canoe into the water. Bill weighed only 135 pounds and as soon as he let go of the canoe he sank in spite of his life jacket. Too late to turn back, he managed to sputter to the surface and start the camera before he was swept through the rapids, just managing to bounce up once in a while to catch his breath. We got a minute and a half of furious bubbles of yellowish water seen from six inches below the surface, punctuated by glimpses of sky and trees.

After that little misadventure, we put two life jackets on Bill, which gave him enough buoyancy to float above the surface, and we got some good shots.

Using the helmet-mounted camera to get the point-of-view shots of Paul's strokes for Path of the Paddle: Flatwater Doubles.
Old Woman Bay, Lake Superior.

The point-of-view camera with its lead counterweight.
Old Woman Bay, Lake Superior.

The bird's-eye-view shot: the high tripod

The engineers in the NFB camera department designed and built this high tripod mount to shoot straight down on the paddler. The engineers loved it when they saw Bill coming; they knew he had some unusual request to challenge them.

We needed this overhead angle to clearly demonstrate the different paddling strokes. It was impossible to shoot from a fixed shooting platform, such as a bridge, because the canoe moved while the strokes were being demonstrated, and of course, then the canoe would no longer be directly beneath the camera.

This rig gave us some important bird's-eye-view shots, however, the camera waved around so much every time the canoe moved that useful shots were very short. We used the 16-mm Beaulieu with 100-foot loads on this mount.

These shots inspired the title, *Path of the Paddle*. When we we were editing, we kept commenting on how well these shots showed the "path of the paddle." Suddenly we both knew that we had the perfect title that had eluded us for so long.

We changed film in the Beaulieu by bringing the canoe over to our shooting rock and tipping the camera toward me. I would take the camera off, reload and remount it. Each time we checked for aperture and focus. Old Woman Bay, Lake Superior.

The bird's-eye-view camera looked straight down into 10 to 40 feet of perfectly clear water in Old Woman Bay, Lake Superior.

The waterproof camera

Bill needed a waterproof camera when he shot *Paddle to the Sea*. He couldn't afford to buy one, nor at the time could he get one from the National Film Board. So Bill made a waterproof housing for his old Kodak CinéSpecial.

He started with an army surplus watertight ammunition box, fitting a little wooden platform in the box to hold the camera in place. Next, he cut a hole in the end of the ammunition box and glued in a #85 filter. Then he made a hole for a plunger to push the button to start the camera. The casing is still 100% waterproof 40 years later.

We used this waterproof casing several times while shooting the canoe series. The old CinéSpecial had incredibly good Ektagraph lenses, so the shots were of good quality. Its only drawbacks were it was awkward and time-consuming to use. The camera held only 100 feet of film, lasting three minutes. To change film or the aperture, we took the whole thing apart, made the change and put it back together—about ten minutes, and by that time the light could have changed. But the camera and casing proved to be dependable workhorses. The camera, a wind-up motor, still works today, whereas the batteries for the Beaulieu died years ago, rendering the camera useless, unless the batteries are replaced at great cost.

We used the waterproof camera to get closeups of Bill as he washed through huge rapids. We wanted the audience to see the terror on his face as he roller-coasted down the rapids. We built a little raft out of plywood and Styrofoam to attach the camera. Extending out from the bottom of the raft was a hockey stick handle, about four feet long. Bill held onto the hockey stick so the raft and camera were always pointing at him and he was in focus. This low-tech rig worked beautifully.

This was my first filming trip with Bill and also the first time I ran rapids while shooting. When Bill explained what we were going to do, I thought he was crazy, but I didn't say a word. I just thought to myself: "I sure hope he knows what he's doing." There was no viewfinder for the waterproof camera, so I pointed it at our subject and hoped for the best. French River, 1970.

Floating through rapids with the waterproof camera. We spent a lot of time at Blue Chute on the French River, where it was relatively easy to set up the camera in several locations on shore. The water was usually deep enough that we did not have to worry about hitting rocks while doing shots like these. For editing purposes, we shot many takes with the camera pointing downstream and upstream. The sequence in Waterwalker *was very dramatic.*

Recording sound: Bev Davidson and Alan Geldart

We shot most of our footage without synchronized sound. We recorded "wild" sound at every location, cutting it into the film later. But we did need to shoot synchronized sound for some sequences, especially the family film, *Song of the Paddle*. Bev Davidson, a professional soundman for the National Film Board, was welcomed as a new member of our crew. Bev's good nature and professionalism put us all at ease when it came time to deliver spontaneous and scripted lines. We were all amateurs when it came to sound recording. Bev patiently led me through the drill. The Masons, with their constant bantering and kibitzing, clammed up when the camera and tape recorder started to roll. Soon Bev had them relaxed and laughing as they learned to pretend that he wasn't there.

Bill hired Alan Geldart to record sound effects for *Waterwalker*. Bill wanted authentic sound whenever possible, not canned stuff from the sound library. So Bill and Alan went back to every major location to capture the sounds of falls, rapids and waves. They spent hours recording different paddle stroke sounds since each stroke makes its own distinctive sound.

The final tracks of music, sound effects and commentary were assembled by professional sound editors at the NFB, notably John Knight and Ken Page.

Getting, and staying, wet

We were never really dry. It just wasn't worth the effort to avoid getting wet. Often I stepped into the water first thing in the morning to get my feet wet so I wouldn't think about it for the rest of the day. There was just too much going on to be thinking about dry feet. During the heat of summer, being wet was not a problem, but in the spring and fall it could be cold and miserable. It was such a relief after a day's shooting to put on dry clothes and shoes, which were packed away in homemade watertight bags. The trouble was we usually shot—and stayed wet—until dusk, so the dry clothes were a heaven-sent luxury for that brief period between the end of the work day and going to bed. On longer trips, I packed a new pair of cotton socks, with the label still on them. Late in the trip I yanked them out of the pack, ripped off the label with great fanfare, and pulled them on my cold, wet feet. This small luxury, and a cup of hot chocolate, restored my spirits for another day.

Anything for that dramatic low angle! I spent a lot of time in the water, and amazingly, we didn't lose a camera or a battery while shooting like this. I once dropped a 400-foot Éclair magazine into a lake. It was only in the water for three or four seconds, but we didn't use it again fearing it wouldn't work properly. Fortunately we had a backup.

Once again Bill takes the plunge for the sake of a shot. This time at the Natch on the Petawawa River.

We often wore hip waders to get low angles. We wore them on Lake Superior because the water was so cold. In this pond in Gatineau Park, hip waders were a defence against blood suckers and muck.

Drying out after shooting in the rain all afternoon. The fire threw enough heat into the Baker tent and under the canopy to dry clothes while it was still raining. Georgian Bay, 1973.

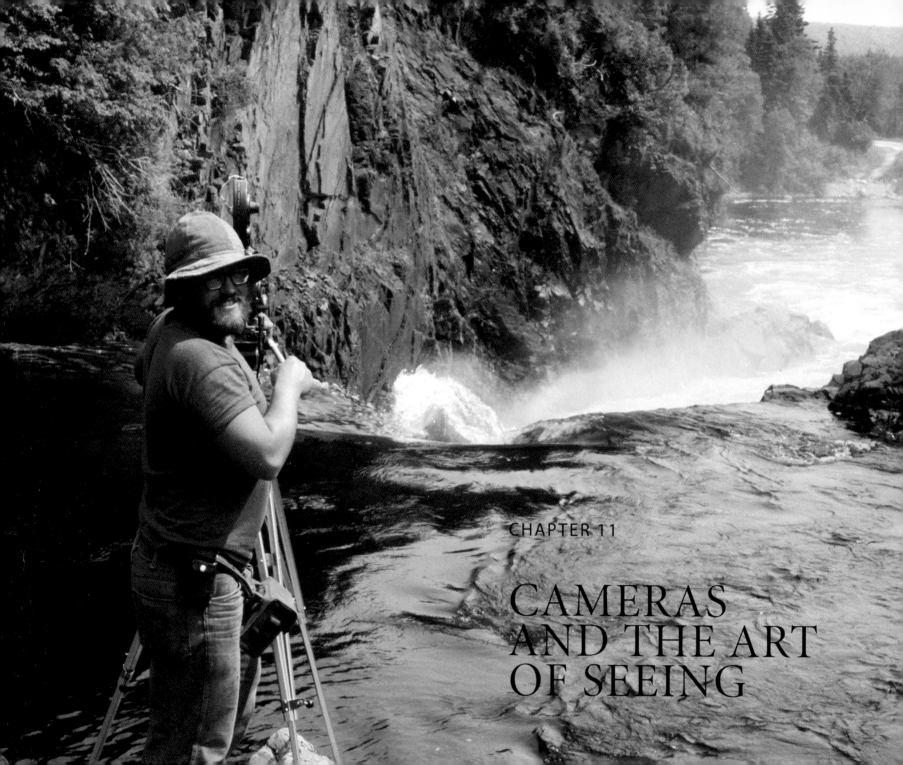

CHAPTER 11

CAMERAS
AND THE ART
OF SEEING

The greatest trick that Bill taught me about being an photographer was "seeing." Bill could see what I could not. He'd look at a panoramic view and say it was boring. Later, under different lighting conditions, he'd remark on how interesting the same view had become. I learned to see with his artistic criteria.

One of the best ways to learn to see is by looking through a camera's viewfinder. When I first started to shoot for Bill, he'd describe a shot he wanted and tell me approximately where to put the camera. I would set the camera up on the tripod and use the viewfinder to frame the shot. He'd then look through the viewfinder to critique my choice. At the beginning, in spite of my attempts to take into account lighting and composition, it was obvious that I had a lot to learn. Sometimes I was annoyed that he would reject my set-up, but his choice was always better when I looked through the viewfinder. We'd discuss exactly what was right or wrong. Over time I got better and better at seeing. In the latter days of our work together we both enjoyed the fact that I could do the set-ups just as well as Bill.

"You push the button. We do the rest."

Kodak slogan, George Eastman, 1888.

LEFT Extreme back lighting on the Petawawa. Normally a photographer uses a fill light, a reflector or a fill flash to bring out details in the shadows. But we had to rely on natural bounce-light reflecting off the water to give details in the shadows, especially on the face.

RIGHT Shooting on the Magpie River near Wawa, Ontario.

Looking through the viewfinder

Wading above the falls on the Magpie River in extreme back lighting.

Using dappled light on the Magpie River to highlight the white in the falls and the red in the canoe.

These production stills, taken with a Nikon 35-mm camera and Rolleiflex medium-format camera, are representative of our use of lighting and composition. We always pushed the capabilities of the film stock, shooting with Kodak 7252 reversal 16-mm film. It was 25 ASA, balanced for indoor use so we needed to compensate with a #85 orange filter, reducing the film speed to 16 ASA. Motion picture cameras operate at 24 frames per second, meaning that the exposure for each frame is about a 55th of a second. This low ASA limited our options when shooting, but the colours were so intense that we were willing to deal with the inconveniences. Film stock has improved remarkably since 1969, but of course, video and digital cameras have made the whole question of ASA almost anachronistic and moot.

It was an ongoing joke that Bill would do anything to get his camera set up in the most difficult places, like the tops of cliffs. All he had to do was ask me to do it, and while he rested in the bottom of the canoe, I climbed the cliff or waterfall or sand-dune or whatever.

To a large degree the joke was based on truth. For my part, I really enjoyed the challenge of getting to a difficult vantage point for the angle that would make a shot especially dramatic, or beautiful, or meaningful. But the fact that Bill trusted me to do the set-up properly was a real compliment.

When I went back to teaching media studies, I took time to instruct students on how to look through a camera, to really see what was in the viewfinder. It is a revelation when they begin to think of the field of vision as a rectangle divided into four equal fields, with each quadrant making its own contribution to the whole picture. Another trick is to look around in the viewfinder without moving the camera, from corner to corner. This encourages the photographer to understand how things in the viewfinder contribute to, or detract from, the photograph.

Shooting Little Thompson on the Petawawa River—we exposed for the whitewater, letting the canoe go black; the dramatic composition makes the canoe seem vulnerable in the whitewater.

On the Petawawa River, the camera was a few inches above the surface of the calm water just above a falls. This low angle resulted in a dramatic shot, especially when Bill stood up. The black background, complemented by back lighting, completed the drama. We exposed for the whitewater and let the shadows on the canoeist go black, creating a halo effect.

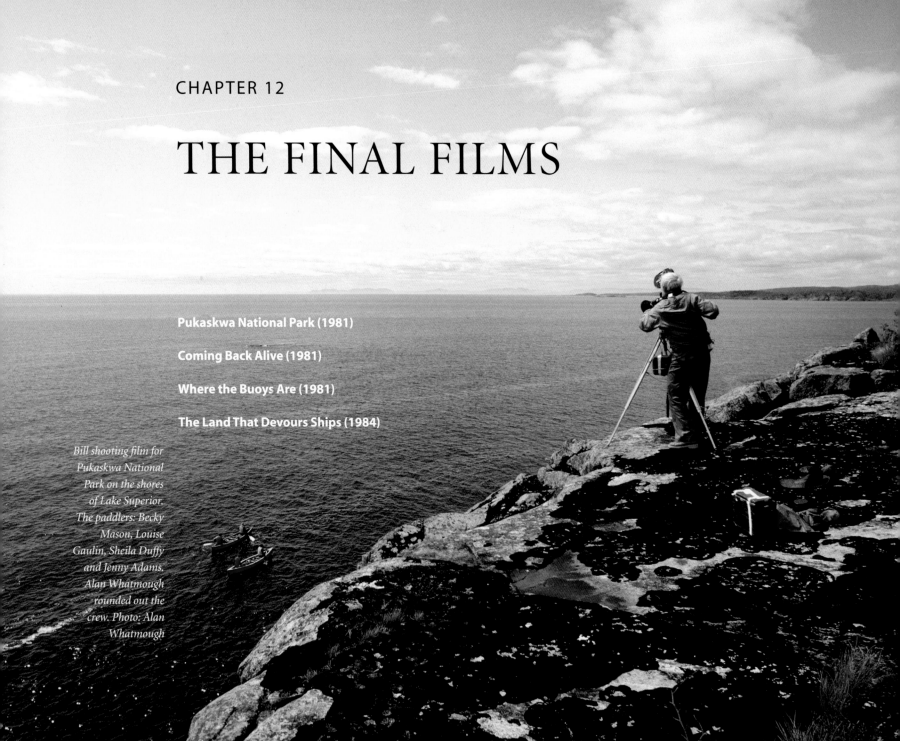

CHAPTER 12

THE FINAL FILMS

Pukaskwa National Park (1981)

Coming Back Alive (1981)

Where the Buoys Are (1981)

The Land That Devours Ships (1984)

Bill shooting film for Pukaskwa National Park on the shores of Lake Superior. The paddlers: Becky Mason, Louise Gaulin, Sheila Duffy and Jenny Adams. Alan Whatmough rounded out the crew. Photo: Alan Whatmough

PUKASKWA NATIONAL PARK (1981)
COMING BACK ALIVE (1981)
WHERE THE BUOYS ARE (1981)

Bill took a leave of absence from the National Film Board from 1977 to 1980 to paint, make up his mind about his future and take a well-deserved rest after completing the canoe project. During this time Bill wrote *Path of the Paddle*, which complements the films. He continued to dream about making a canoe feature, writing scripts and outlines for it. He edited the canoe out-takes into a first draft, trying to interest the NFB and other producers, but no one was willing to put up the money to finish the feature. By 1980 Bill was at a crossroads: retire from the NFB to paint, or, as an NFB employee, make films about topics that did not really interest or appeal to him.

Until 1980 Bill had initiated his own film projects. He really wanted to make those films and they were extensions of him. The completion of the canoe films had exhausted his to-do list of films. He was at a loss as to what new topic he could make with the same enthusiasm.

I was aghast at Bill's plan to leave filmmaking to pursue painting. From my point of view, Bill had aroused the imagination and loyalty of hundreds of thousands of devotees as a powerful spokesperson for environmental causes. In my mind, he was the one person—an icon—who could ignite positive changes in environmental problems, many of which were not as palatable and saleable as wilderness stewardship. I remember debating with Bill about whether or not he should retire from filmmaking. He asked me what topic I thought he should tackle next if he continued as a filmmaker. I suggested a difficult environmental problem such as landfills and waste management, perhaps done in the style of *Rise and Fall of the Great Lakes*. It was Bill's turn to be aghast. There was no way.

When he returned to the NFB in 1980, he was assigned three films—*Pukaskwa National Park*, *Coming Back Alive* and *Where the Buoys Are*. Bill completed these films in the highest professional manner, but they did not ignite the old enthusiasm. Bill continued to try to sell his idea about a canoe feature, but the NFB remained adamant. They were not interested.

Bill made some life-altering decisions: he would retire from the National Film Board; he would make a canoe feature using the out-takes from *Path of the Paddle* with, or without, the NFB's backing; he would write another instructional book based on *Song of the Paddle* to complement the instructional film; and he would paint. Remarkably, he accomplished all these goals, and more, in the too-short time he had left.

These decisions proved to be best for Bill, who thrived in his newfound freedom. He began to take more canoe trips with friends. He wrote the book *Song of the Paddle*. He marshalled enough money to make and launch the canoe feature *Waterwalker*. He wrote a book about his paintings, *Canoescapes*, which he finished, literally, on his deathbed. But most importantly, he painted. Finally nothing stood between him and his easel. The daunting task of fulfilling his life-long dream was the only task left. One of the greatest challenges of his life began.

Bill shooting film for Pukaskwa National Park on the shores of Lake Superior. Photo by Jeff Schmarr.

THE LAND THAT DEVOURS SHIPS (1984)

Dr. Joe MacInnis persuaded Bill to come out of retirement in 1983 for one more film. He and Bill had collaborated in 1974 on the NFB film, *In Search of the Bowhead Whale,* and had been good friends since then. Joe, trained as a physician, had made quite a name for himself as a diver, especially in extreme conditions. He was a good friend of Pierre Trudeau, moving comfortably in the halls of power and money. He dove at the North Pole with both Trudeau and Prince Charles.

Joe was interested in doing important dives and making documentary films about these adventures. He wanted Bill to make a documentary about high-tech dives on the Breadalbane shipwreck, a ship that was lost in 1846 while searching for Sir John Franklin and his crew just off Beechy Island in the Canadian Arctic. Deep-sea divers, led by Phil Nuytten, were being used on the dive while the National Geographic Society, one of the sponsors for the search, featured the story in its magazine. A documentary film, especially one made by Bill Mason, would give the Canadian diving community great publicity, potentially leading to further funding, and eventually, even more ambitious dives.

The camp on the ice over the wreck of the Breadalbane just off Beechy Island. The blue and white tent covers the CAN-DIVE one-man submarine and powerful winches used to raise and lower it. The tent in the distance covers the robotic cameras and their controls. They were lowered through different holes in the ice so the cameras could film the manned machines without getting their tethers entangled.

Bill had reservations about getting back into film. After all, his canoe feature had not yet been put to bed. Nonetheless he agreed to shoot, direct and edit the film. The National Film Board and Joe MacInnis were co-producers. Bill, once again, did a professional job and was happy with the final product. But the project only confirmed that he did not want to make films, especially if he didn't have complete control.

During the dives Joe approved the retrieval of the Breadalbane's wheel. He rationalized that no one could ever afford to make a recreational dive, or an archeological one, on the wreck again (the project cost about $1 million) so the artifact would better serve the common interests of both Canada and the United States in a museum, rather than at the bottom of the Arctic Ocean.

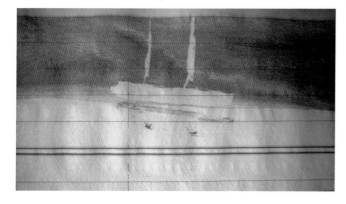

The Breadalbane was located using side-scan sonar. Looking for a wreck in the Arctic Ocean is a needle-in-a-haystack exercise. But the research said that the wreck should be in a particular bay. A side-scan sonar unit was dragged across the bay in a methodical grid, eventually getting an image of the intact wreck. This discovery confirmed that this new technology was capable of making underwater archeological finds. It has been used many more times to find important wrecks.

Inside the dive site tent the crew readies the manned CAN-DIVE robot, called the Wasp, which was lowered 300 feet by winch to photograph the Breadalbane wreck. Once lowered, the Wasp was manoeuvered by a diver to explore the wreck.

CHAPTER 13

THE STUDIO:
A CABIN IN THE
WOODS

Bill's studio is a good place to bring this story to an end. Some of Canada's best documentary films were made in this unpretentious, plywood-sided cottage. It was palatial compared to the tiny quarters in the house where Bill had his first studio, and it was his sanctuary. Seldom was anyone invited in; Bill always went to the house to meet visitors, summoned by a preset signal when Joyce, his first line of defence, turned the electricity off and on.

Bill made editing look easy, but few people saw the endless hours of painstaking construction that went into every scene. All the cutting was done with scissors, with the pieces assembled with a specialized Scotch tape. Compared to today's digital editing, it was stone-age technology. At first the NFB was reluctant to give Bill a high-tech flatbed editing machine, a Steenbeck, for the studio. Their reluctance was understandable since the machine was worth well over $100,000 in 1975, and they did not have enough other Steenbecks at headquarters in Montreal. But Bill's persistence, his record of successful films and the sheer volume of his productivity convinced management that it was a legitimate request. After the Steenbeck arrived, our productivity increased dramatically.

Bill was in many ways a one-man operation, except when it came to music. He wanted hands-on control of everything in his films. When the credits roll his name appears again and again: director, cinematography, picture editing, titles graphics, animation. But when it came to music Bill bowed to the authority of Larry Crosley who composed and arranged the music for most of Bill's films. Larry arrived late in the editing process, transforming the films with his scores. It was a great day when we first saw the picture with his music.

Just the sheer volume of footage meant that Bill needed an assistant editor for the canoe project. I consider the editing that I did for him, and with him, to have been one of the great learning experiences of my life. Editing the rushes that I had shot taught me more about shooting and directing film than anything else.

But editing also taught me so much about the importance of stories in defining who we are. John Grierson, the first director of the NFB, had a vision of telling Canadians their own stories through films made by a filmmaking company owned by Canadians. The National Film Board became a cornerstone in making Canada a strong nation. In my four years studying English and history at university, I was caught up in the timeless stories without realizing that they expressed and shaped reality at the same time. Until I edited films, I did not appreciate the role of the artist-storyteller who constructed stories for a nation. Until the day of this writing, I never, even for a moment, take for granted the privilege it was to spend hundreds of hours working in the wilderness and in that studio with Bill Mason.

How appropriate that some of Canada's greatest stories were dreamed and shaped in that little cabin in the woods.

. . .

CLOCKWISE
Bill at the Steenbeck, a flatbed editing machine. Me at the editing table. Bill working with a viewer doing a rough cut before using the Steenbeck to do a fine cut with sound.

BILL MASON: FILMOGRAPHY/BIBLIOGRAPHY

WILDERNESS TREASURE

(Manitoba Pioneer Camps) 20 minutes: researched, directed, filmed, edited, 1959-1962.

1) First Prize, Travel and Recreation Category, Canadian Film Awards, May 1963.
2) Chris Award, 11th Annual Columbus Film Festival, October 1963.

PADDLE TO THE SEA

(National Film Board 106C 0166 061) 20 minutes: researched, directed, filmed, edited, 1962-1964.

1) First Prize, Stories for Children Category, American Film Festival, New York, 1967.
2) First Prize, Ex-aequo with Germany, Information Films Category, International Festival of 16-mm and 8-mm Films, Salerno, Italy, 1967.
3) Golden Plaque, Educational Films for Children, Second Children's Film Festival, Teheran, Iran, 1967.
4) Best Film, Creative Arts and Experimental Films, 9th International Film Festival, Yorkton, Saskatchewan, 1967.
5) Nominated for Best Short Film, Academy of Motion Picture Arts and Sciences, Hollywood, California, April 8, 1968.
6) Best Documentary Film (Silver Plaque), International Festival of Films for Children, La Plata, Argentina, October 13, 1968.
7) Award for Exceptional Merit, International Festival of Short Films, Philadelphia, Pennsylvania, November 13 - 18, 1971.
8) Certificate of Merit, International Film Review, Colombo, Sri Lanka, September 4 - 10, 1969.
9) Special Award, Montreal Society of Filmmakers, 1966.
10) For the Filmstrip: Silver Medal, Education—Language Arts Category, 30th Annual Awards Competition, International Film and Television Festival, USA, November 13, 1987.

RISE AND FALL OF THE GREAT LAKES

(National Film Board 106C 0168 093)

17 minutes: researched, directed, filmed, edited, animation, 1965-1966.

1) Best Specialized Film, Society of Film and Television Arts, London, England, March 1971.
2) Certificate of Merit and Special Award for the Best Film of the Year, Canadian Amateur Film Association, Montreal, Quebec, May 1971.
3) Diploma of Merit, 1st International Film Festival on the Human Environment, Montreal, Quebec, June 1 - 10, 1973.
4) First Place, Documentary Category, 8th International Festival of Documentary and Experimental Films, Montevideo, Uruguay, July 2, 1971.
5) Winsted Rotary Club Award to Canada for the Best Movie, 2nd International Environmental Pollution Exhibition, Winsted, Connecticut, October 25, 1975.
6) Certificate of Merit, 1st International Film Festival, Tel Aviv, Israel, 1969.
7) Prize, Educational Category, 10th International Yorkton Film Festival, 1969.
8) Blue Ribbon, 12th American Film Festival, New York, 1970.
9) Silver Water Bucket Plaque, San Francisco Water Pollution Conference, 1970.
10) First Prize, Scientific Category, 6th International Scientific, Educational and Pedagogical Films, Teheran, Iran, 1969.

BLAKE

(National Film Board 106C 0169 076) 20 minutes: researched, directed, edited, 1967.

1) Accepted, Society of Film and Television Arts, London, England, March 1971.

2) Etrog, Best Film under 30 minutes, Canadian Film Awards, Toronto, October 3, 1970.

3) Golden Sheaf Award, Best Direction, International Film Festival, Yorkton, Saskatchewan, October 18 - 23, 1971.

4) Golden Sheaf Award, Best Social Science Film, International Film Festival, Yorkton, Saskatchewan, October 18 - 23, 1971.

5) Grand Prix, Golden Boomerang, Melbourne Film Festival, Melbourne, Australia, June 4-19, 1971.

6) Nominated Best Live Action Short Film, Annual Academy of Motion Picture Arts and Sciences, Hollywood, California, April 1970.

DEATH OF A LEGEND

(National Film Board 106C 0171 553) 52 minutes: researched, directed, filmed, edited, animation, 1968.

1) Award for Exceptional Merit, International Festival of Short Films, Philadelphia, Pennsylvania, November 11 - 18, 1971.

2) Diploma of Honour, 2nd International Days of Scientific and Didactic Films, Madrid, Spain, October 1972.

3) Etrog, Best Colour Cinematography, Canadian Film Awards, Toronto, October 1, 1971.

4) Gold Medal, 22nd International Festival for Tourist and Folklore Films, Brussels, Belgium, October 9 - 13, 1972.

5) Golden Rhododendron Award, 22nd International Festival of Exploration and Mountain Films, Trento, Italy, April 1974.

6) Golden Sheaf Award, Best Nature and Wildlife Film, International Film Festival, Yorkton, Saskatchewan, October 15 - 20, 1973.

7) Golden Sheaf Award, Best Cinematography, International Film Festival, Yorkton, Saskatchewan, October 15 - 20, 1973.

8) Red Ribbon Award, 14th American Film Festival, New York, May 9 - 13, 1972.

9) For Au Pays des Loups (French Translation): Coupe du Ministre des spectacles, 8e festival international de films pour enfants et adolescents, Salerno, Italy, July 1978.

WOLF PACK

(National Film Board 106C 0174 501) 20 minutes: researched, directed, filmed, edited, 1971.

1) Best Film in the Professional Category, University of Montana, Missoula, Montana, April 1978.

2) Award given by *Learning Magazine*, Palo Alto, California, 1978.

3) Coupe du Ministre des spectacles, 8e festival international de films pour enfants et adolescents, Salerno, Italy, July, 1978.

IN SEARCH OF THE BOWHEAD WHALE

(National Film Board 106C 0174 094) 52 minutes: researched, directed, filmed, edited, animation, commentary and narration, 1974.

1) Blue Ribbon Award, Environment, Nature and Wildlife Category, 17th American Film Festival, New York, June 2 - 17, 1975.

2) Chris Award, 24th International Film Festival, Columbus, Ohio, October 21, 1976.

3) First Award for Best Film in the Exploration Discovery Category, Black Orca Film Festival, Seattle, Washington, June 14 - 15, 1978.

4) Highest Merit in the Invited non-1977 films Category, University of Montana, Missoula, Montana, April 1978.

5) Silver Venus Medallion: Best Film in the TV Documentary Category, International Film Festival, US Virgin Islands, November 7 - 16, 1975.

6) Jules Verne Award for Best Exploration Film, First International Festival of Films on the Arctic, Dieppe, France, June 3 - 5, 1983.

CRY OF THE WILD

(National Film Board 106C 0172 015) 90 minutes: researched, directed, filmed, acted, edited, graphics, commentary and narration, 1968-1971.

1) Diploma of Merit, 1st International Film Festival of the Human Environment, Montreal, 1973.

FACE OF THE EARTH

(National Film Board 106C 175 109) 20 minutes: researched, directed, filmed, edited, 1975.

1) Blue Ribbon Award, Category 9: Elementary/Junior High Curriculum Films—Science, 19th Annual American Film Festival, New York, May 23 - 28, 1977.

2) Certificate of Recognition, Clarity and Correlation to Curriculum Area, Instructional Film Festival, Cleveland, Ohio, January, 1980.

PATH OF THE PADDLE: SOLO BASIC

(National Film Board 106C 0177 008) 27 minutes: researched, directed,acted,edited,animation,commentaryandnarration,1976.

PATH OF THE PADDLE: SOLO WHITEWATER

(National Film Board 106C 0177 009) 27 minutes: researched, directed, acted, edited, animation, commentary and narration, 1976.

1) Best Script Film, First International Contest for White Water Films, Venissieux, France, May 1983.

PATH OF THE PADDLE: DOUBLES BASIC

(National Film Board 106C 0177 010) 27 minutes: researched, directed,acted,edited,animation,commentaryandnarration,1976.

PATH OF THE PADDLE: DOUBLES WHITEWATER

(National Film Board 106C 0177 011) 27 minutes: researched, directed, acted, edited, animation, commentary and narration, 1976.

1) Best Specialized Film, British Academy of Film and Television Arts, London, March 16, 1978.

2) Chris Bronze Plaque, Education Category, 26th International Film Festival, Columbus, Ohio, October 19, 1978.

3) Grand Prix of the Cultural Ministry of Nordrhein-Westfalen (cash award 5,000 DM), International Sport Film Festival, Oberhausen, West Germany, October 24 - 28, 1977.

4) Special Jury Award for Outstanding Achievement, Film as Communication Competition, 21st Annual International Film Festival, San Francisco, California, October 5 - 16, 1977.

5) For French Version: Prix. CIDALC Renee Barthelemy, 9e festival international CIDALC du film sportif, Rennes, France, May 1982.

6) Prix decerne au meilleur film a scenario (cash award 2,000 francs). Premier festival international du film de descente de riviere, Venissieux, France, May 1983.

SONG OF THE PADDLE

(National Film Board 106C 0178 111) 41 minutes: researched, directed, acted, edited, commentary and narration, 1976.

1) ANICA Award, 10th International Cinema Festival for Children and Young People, Salerno, Italy, July, 1980.

2) Award from the Tourist Bureau of the Veneto, 2nd International Adventure Film Festival, Cortina d'Ampezzo, Italy, July 20 - 25, 1980.

3) Chris Award, Travel Category, 28th Annual International Film Festival, Columbus, Ohio, October 23, 1980.

4) Etrog, Best Direction, Canadian Film Awards, Toronto, September 14 - 21, 1978.

5) Etrog, Best Cinematography in Documentary under 60 Minutes (Cinematographer, Ken Buck), Canadian Film Awards, Toronto, September 14 - 21, 1978.

6) Etrog, Best Sound Editing (Sound Editors, John Knight and Ken Page), Canadian Film Awards, Toronto, September 14 - 21, 1978.

7) Honourable Mention, 4th Annual Festival of Mountain Films, Banff, Alberta, November 1979.

8) Best Tourism Film, 29th International Festival for Tourist and Folklore Films, Brussels, Belgium, October 1979.

9) Red Ribbon Award, Nature and Wildlife Category, 21st Annual American Film Festival, New York, May 1979.

When the Wolves Sang (Greey de Pencier), 1980.

DRAGON CASTLE (Bill Mason Productions) 13 minutes: produced, 15 International Awards to Paul and Becky Mason, 1980.

Path of the Paddle (Van Nostrand Reinhold), 1980. (Key Porter Books), 1984. Second edition published with text updated by Paul Mason (Key Porter Books), 1995.

COMING BACK ALIVE (National Film Board 1 0180 037), 1980.

PUKASKWA NATIONAL PARK (National Film Board 106C 0183 553) 16 minutes: directed, filmed, edited and commentary, 1981.

WHERE THE BUOYS ARE (National Film Board) 1981.

L'aviron Qui Nous Mene (French translation of *Path of the Paddle* published by Marcel Broquet in Quebec), 1981.

THE LAND THAT DEVOURS SHIPS (National Film Board 106C 0184 073) 58 minutes: directed, filmed, edited, animation and narration, 1984.
1) Special Jury Award, 3rd International Festival of Films on Art and Archaeology, Brussels, Belgium, February 1986.

WATERWALKER (National Film Board and Imago) 87 minutes: researched,: directed, acted, edited and narration, 1984.
1) Nature and Environment Award, IVe festival international du film de descente de riviere, Valence, France, November 1989.

Die Kunst des Kannfahrens der Canadier (German translation of *Path of the Paddle* published by BusseSeewalk Herford in West Germany), 1987.

Song of the Paddle (Key Porter Books), 1988.

Canoescapes (Boston Mills Press (Stoddart)), 1995.

Relevant Filmography

Bonisteel, Roy
The Genial Fanatic, Man Alive, CBC (1988)

Chapman, Chris
http://www.scugog-net.com/chapman/

A Place to Stand Expo '67, Ontario Pavilion
A Sense of Humus, Organic Farming
Bluenose II, Maiden Voyage of the reproduction of the original Bluenose
Enduring Wilderness, The
Kelly (1981)
Magic Molecule, The (1964)
Persistent Seed, The (1964)
Quetico (1958)
Seasons, The
Science North Sudbury, 3-D science film
Expo '70 Japan, Ontario Pavilion

Ellis, Ralph
Keg Productions
Spirit of Wilderness (1989)

Gosnell, Larry
Air of Death, CBC (1967)

Relevant Readings

Carson, Rachel
Silent Spring (1962)

Holling, Holling C.
Paddle-to-the-Sea. Houghton Mifflin Company, Boston (1941, 1969)

Meadows, Donella, et al., Club of Rome
Limits to Growth (1972)
Limits to Growth: Thirty Years Later (2001)

Olsen, Sigurd
Listening Point (1958)
The Lonely Land (1961)
Of Time and Place (1982)
Open Horizons (1969)
Reflections from the North Country/Sigurd F. Olsen; ill. by Leslie Kouba (1976)
Runes of the North (1963)
The Singing Wilderness; illus. by Francis Lee Jaques (1956)

Raffan, James
Fire In the Bones—Bill Mason and the Canadian Canoeing Tradition (1996). A Phyllis Bruce Book. Published by Harper Collins

Rutstrum, Calvin
The New Way of the Wilderness (1958)
North American Canoe Country (1964)
Once Upon a Wilderness (1973)
Paradise Below Zero (1968)
The Wilderness Cabin/Calvin Rutstrum; illustrated by Les Kouba (1961).
The Wilderness Route Finder (1967)

INDEX

A

Academy Award, 12, 143, 160
After the Game, 21
Air of Death (1967), 163
Alexander, Mel, 10, 28
Allied Van Lines, 48
animation, 72-9, 123, 178, 215
art, following the masters, 94
    life drawing, 96-7
    oil paint to paper, 192
    painting in the field, 108
    palette knife, 12, 94, 108-111, 192
    sketchbook, 93-95, 109-110-117, 137

B

Becky, Rebecca Joy (Becky) (daughter), 4, 8-9, 27, 30-31,
    50, 73, 79, 82, 108, 134, 156, 171, 180, 183, 210, 219
Beechy Island, 212
Bice, Ralph, 176
Blake, 12, 18, 24, 29, 50, 132, 139, 143, 144, 147, 152-161,
    164, 166, 174
Blake, William, Romantic poet, 29
Blue Chute, 183, 198, 203
bowhead whale, 163, 177
Brault, Louise, 184
Breadalbane, 212-213
Brown, Derek, 185
Brown, Robin, 185
Bryant. Barry, 198
Buck, Ian, 29
Buck, Jenny, 29
Buck, Ken, 3, 10, 125, 180, 215, 219
Buck, Susan, 8-9, 180, 184-185, 198
Burr, Bill, 8

C

cameras, # 85 filter, 203, 208
    16-mm Arriflex, 197
    16-mm Éclair, 192, 197, 205
    16-mm Kodak CinéSpecial, 71-73, 78, 149, 192-203
    16-mm Beaulieu, 125, 195-7, 202-3
    and the art of seeing, 12, 29, 71, 182, 206-7
    batteries, 177, 197, 203
    black bag, 198-9
    camera equipment, 195-7
    film stock, 7252 reversal 16-mm, 208
    floating, 147, 149, 158, 178, 200, 203
    helmet, 201
    high tripod, 202
    loading and unloading films, 198-9
    Nikon 35-mm, 208
    Nikon lenses, 24-mm, 300-mm, 600-mm, 125, 169,
        171, 195-6, 208
    Rolleiflex, 11, 24, 55-6, 208
    waterproof, 147, 149, 192, 198, 201, 203
Campbell, Don, 8, 24, 37, 50, 55-56, 73, 78
camping, family wilderness, 180
    living outdoors, 65
    Red River, first time camping, 17
    safe canoeing, 181
CAN-DIVE, 212-13
canoeing, sailing, 23, 27, 184
Carey, Miss (art teacher), 15, 33
Carson, Rachel, author if *The Silent Spring*, 163, 219
Cartooning, 18, 80-91
Cascade Falls, 25, 191-192
catamaran, 174, 184, 199-200
Chapman, Chris, 12, 50, 73, 139, 143, 165
Christianity, 11, 22-23, 55-56, 140
    decision to drop overt Christian message, 56

Coming Back Alive, 76, 210-11

commercial art, 8, 11-12, 15, 24, 34, 38, 40-53, 58, 64, 151, 171

Crabtree, Grant, 27, 73, 156

Crawley, Budge, (Crawley Film Studios), 10, 21, 26, 73, 89, 160

Crosley, Larry, composer, 178, 180, 215

Cry of the Wild (feature documentary), 10, 126, 139, 160, 162-163, 167, 189

Canadian Wildlife Services, (CWS), 164-165, 167-8, 171

D

dams, 84, 118, 153

Davidson, Bev (soundman), 204

Death of a Legend, 11, 76, 139, 160, 162-167

Denison Falls, University (Dog) River, 4, 190-191, 195, 204

Dennison, Judith, 200

Disney, Walt, 34, 73, 76, 123, 130, 164-165

documentary film, 10, 12, 15, 55, 73, 126, 139, 163-164, 166-167, 177, 189, 195-196, 199, 212, 215
truth in, 26, 126, 136, 166, 195-196, 208

Dog (University) River, 4, 190-1, 195, 204

Dragon Castle, 79, 218

E

editing, 26, 90, 123, 137, 170, 196, 201-203, 215
Steenbeck, 215

Elim Chapel, 22-23, 26, 55

Ellis, Ralph, 167, 219

environment, responsibility, stewardship, 10, 11, 12, 23, 29, 41-42, 45-8, 53, 63, 84, 131-132, 141, 144, 163-164

environmentalists, 12, 131, 176

F

Face of the Earth, 11, 75, 139, 178

Fair, Thomas (maternal grandfather) Grampa, 16, 23

faith, Christian, 11, 22, 56

Franklin, Sir John, 212

French River, 9, 181-183, 198, 203

G

Gatineau Park, 148, 160, 163, 167, 183, 205

Geldart, Alan (soundman), 204

Genial Fanatic, Man Alive, CBC, 70

Georgian Bay, 7-9, 30-1, 55, 59, 93, 101, 131, 141, 180-182, 196, 205

God's Grandeur, slide show, early 1950s, 24, 55-6

Gosnell, Larry, (filmmaker), *Air of Death*, 163

Grand Beach, 16, 18, 23, 33, 37

Great Lakes, 48, 76, 143, 153, 181, 185

Greeting cards, 81-91

Grierson, John, first director of the NFB, 215

H

Herman, Blake, 18

hockey, 18, 20-22, 28, 33, 41, 81, 83, 149, 203

Holling C, Holling, author of *Paddle-to-the-Sea*, 73, 143, 219

Hubbs, Cam, 168

hydroelectric power, 84, 118

I

In Search of the Bowhead Whale, 139, 164, 177, 212, 217

Inter-Varsity Christian Fellowship, 22-3, 140

J

Jacques, Francis Lee, illustrator, 24
James, Blake, 24, 132, 143, 147, 153, 160, 166, 174
Jaws, 24, 132, 143-4, 147, 152-61, 166, 174

K

kayak, homemade, 16-17
KEG Productions, 167, 189
Kelvin High School, 19, 22, 33
Kodak, 9, 71, 73, 78, 149, 192, 203, 207-8

L

Lake Superior, 8, 25, 29, 56, 120, 125, 130, 132-133, 135,
        144, 148, 153-154, 158, 175, 181, 187-188, 190-191,
        198, 199-202, 204-205, 210
Land Rover, 50, 144
lenses, 12-mm to 120-mm zoom Angenieux, 195
        24-mm, 300-mm, Nikon lenses, 195
        600-mm, 125, 169, 171, 195-196
        Ektagraph, 203
Land that Devours Ships, The, 139, 210, 212, 219
Litteljohn, Bruce, 200, 204

M

MacInnis, Dr. Joe, 177, 212-213
Magnetawan River, 183, 198
Magpie River, 149, 207-8
Manitoba Pioneer Camp, 23, 26, 33, 58, 140, 150
maple syrup, making maple syrup at Meech Lake, 27, 44
maps, 25, 55, 76
Mason, Bill (William Clifford)
        and politics, 44

and the logging industry, 42
celebrity status, 11
Christianity, religion and life at home, 22
environmentalism as a political movement, 165
finding his artist's voice, 34
health problems, 18, 24, 50, 164
leave of absence from the NFB, 211
painting as a new full time career, 211
professional painter, 12
retirement from the NFB, 42, 211
romantic persona, 11
teacher, 8, 15, 23, 33
teaching, 9, 10-11, 23, 29, 180,
the artist as a student, 33
Turning point: 1967 - 1970, 163
wedding, 26
Mason, Elizabeth (paternal grandmother) Granny, 22
Mason, Elizabeth Catherine (sister) MacKenzie, 8, 12,
        15, 33, 163
Mason, Loraine Joyce (wife) nee Ferguson, 8, 10, 26-28,
        30, 33, 38, 44, 50, 53, 86, 89, 129, 134, 169-171, 180,
        182, 215
Mason, Paul David (son), 8-9, 21, 27, 30-31, 42, 50, 53,
        73, 79, 82, 89, 146, 156, 171, 180, 185, 187, 201, 219
Mason, Sadie (mother) nee Fair, 15, 22, 24
Mason, William Thomas (Bill, Sr., father), 15-16, 22, 33
McKay, Bruce, composer/musician, 153
McKenzie, Elizabeth Catherine (sister), 8, 15, 33
Meech Lake, 9-10, 17, 20-22, 26-28, 41, 50, 73, 86, 90,
        152, 155-156, 160, 163, 168, 172, 175, 184, 196
Meldrum, Joey, 29
Meldrum, Peter, 29
Mitchell, Dr. Fred, 22-23
music, Bruce Cockburn, 189
        Marsh, Hugh, 189

Campbell, David, 180
  Nexus, 178
  The Canadian Brass, 178
  Weissburg, Eric, 178

N

National Film Board of Canada (NFB), 9, 11-12, 42, 73,
    96, 141, 143, 153, 160, 163-164, 166, 180, 185, 189,
    195, 200-204, 211-213, 215, 217-220
Nelson Boat Livery, 16
Nelson, Barrie, 24, 50
Niagara Falls, 126, 143, 147-148
Nuytten, Phil, 212

O

Old Woman Bay, 125, 133, 135, 153, 187, 198-204
Olsen, Sigurd, author of *The Singing Wilderness*, 24
Oscar, Academy Award nomination, 9, 22, 139, 143, 167

P

Paddle to the Sea, 11-12, 48, 73, 76, 132, 139, 142-145,
    147, 153, 158, 160, 163-164, 203
Path of the Paddle (series of four instructional films), 9,
    11, 75-76, 90, 125, 139, 160, 179-180, 185, 187, 189-
    190, 201-202, 211, 219-20
Paul, Phelan and Perry Ltd., 26, 42, 53
Petawawa River, 124, 137, 205, 207-209
Phillips, Gutkin and Associates, 24, 42, 55, 78
photography, back lighting, 60, 207-209
    bounce-light, 207
    composition, 9, 55-58, 64, 94, 182, 207-208
    extreme lighting, 70

light, the use of light in, 69
lighting, 55-8, 136, 154, 188, 207-208
    still, 12
    the art of Seeing, 71, 81
    the silhouette, 64
    use of the tripod, 62, 70-71, 125, 136, 154, 188, 192,
        196, 202, 207
Picanoc River, 48, 186
Pimlott, Dr. Douglas, 165
pollution, 65, 131-2, 143, 153, 158
Pollution Probe, 163
Prince Charles, 212
Prince Philip, 163
Pukaskwa National Park, 76, 139, 191, 210-211

Q

Queen Elizabeth, 12, 163
Quetico, 12, 73, 139, 165, 219

R

Raffan, James, 8, 41, 53, 219
Reimer Express, 41, 46-8, 74, 78
Rise and Fall of the Great Lakes, 11, 75-76, 126, 132, 139,
    152-153, 157-158, 160, 164, 211
Riverview Community Centre, 20-21
Royal Academy of Arts, 12
Rutstrum, Calvin, author, 24-25, 66, 219

S

Schaber, Wally, 8, 21
Schultz, Charles M., 81
Seaman, Lloyd, 8

Selwyn, Dave, 197
Selwyn, John, 185
Shoal Lake, 23, 26, 139
Song of the Paddle, 23, 76, 135, 139, 179-184, 190, 204,
    211, 220
Star Weekly, Saturday supplement to the *Toronto Star*,
    25, 191
storyboards, 96, 122-6
    shattering the Hollywood stereotype, 126
    using storyboards in the field, 135
studio, the, 8, 10, 12, 26, 55, 72-3, 76, 93, 108, 124, 170,
    214-5
Sutherland, Wilber, 23, 189

T

Tabernacle, 73, 78-9
tectonic plates, 75, 178
tent, Baker (campfire tent, reflector tent, Bill Mason
    tent), 9, 11, 24-25, 66-67, 125, 163, 205
Timeless Wilderness, The, slide show (early 1950s), 12,
    55-57, 67, 71, 139, 161
Thomson, Tom, 24, 34, 41, 60
Trailhead, 8
transcendentalism, 29
Trudeau, Margaret, 163
Trudeau, Pierre Elliott (Prime Minister), 12, 44, 90, 163-
    164, 212
Turner, J.M.W. (William), 38, 69, 94-95, 108

U

United Grain Growers, 44-45
University of Manitoba, 11, 15, 18, 78

V

Voyageurs, The, 76, 139, 141
voyageurs, 33, 36, 44, 47, 74, 141

W

Waterwalker (feature documentary), 2, 5, 10, 12, 15, 23-
    24, 56-58, 74, 76, 78, 95, 123-124, 126, 139, 158, 179,
    189-192, 203-204, 211
Whatmough, Alan, 189, 210
Where the Buoys Are, 76, 139, 210-11
wilderness, 9-12, 16, 22-24, 28, 33, 36-38, 41, 45, 50, 55-
    56, 58, 61, 65, 71, 73, 76, 84, 111, 125-127, 129, 133,
    140-141, 164, 166, 176, 180-182, 185, 189, 192, 195-
    197, 211, 215
Wilderness Treasure, 23, 26, 73, 139-40, 189
Wilson, Dr. Tuzo, 178
Wolf Pack, 11, 139, 160, 162, 166-7
wolves, 9, 24, 76, 130, 163-172, 174-175
    cubs, 170-171, 174
    disproved the legend, 175
    enclosure at Meech Lake, 9, 163, 165, 168-172, 174-175
    Isle Royale, 175
    wanton killer legend, 166
Wright, Dave, 155, 163, 168

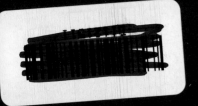